Epworth Commentaries

General Editors
Harold F. Guite and Ivor H. Jones

The Books of Amos and Hosea

The Books of
AMOS & HOSEA

HARRY MOWVLEY

EPWORTH PRESS

Copyright © Harry Mowvley 1991

Extracts from the Revised English Bible are © 1989
by the Delegates of the Oxford University Press
and the Syndics of the Cambridge University Press,
and are used by permission.

British Library Cataloguing in Publication Data

Mowvley, Harry
  The books of Amos & Hosea.
  1. Christianity. Scriptures. Bible. O. T. Amos. Hosea
  I. Title
  224.607
  ISBN 0-7126-0475-4

First published 1991
by Epworth Press
1 Central Buildings Westminster
London SW1H 9NR

Phototypeset by Intype, London
and printed in Great Britain by
Billing and Sons Ltd, Worcester

CONTENTS

HOSEA

GENERAL PREFACE

The *Epworth Preacher's Commentaries* that Greville P. Lewis edited so successfully in the 1950s and 1960s having now served their turn, the Epworth Press has commissioned a team of distinguished academics who are also preachers and teachers to create a new series of commentaries that will serve the 1990s and beyond. We have seized the opportunity offered by the publication in 1989 of the Revised English Bible to use this very readable and scholarly version as the basis of our commentaries, and we are grateful to the Oxford and Cambridge University Presses for the requisite licence and for granting our authors pre-publication access. They will nevertheless be free to cite and discuss other translations wherever they think that these will illuminate the original text.

Just as the books that make up the Bible differ in their provenance and purpose, so our authors will necessarily differ in the structure and bearing of their commentaries. But they will all strive to get as close as possible to the intention of the original writers, expounding their texts in the light of the place, time, circumstance, and culture that gave them birth, and showing why each work was received by Jews and Christians into their respective Canons of Holy Scripture. They will seek to make full use of the dramatic advances in biblical scholarship world-wide but at the same time to explain technical terms in the language of the common reader, and to suggest ways in which Scripture can help towards the living of a Christian life today. They will endeavour to produce commentaries that can be used with confidence in ecumenical, multiracial, and multifaith situations, and not by scholars only but by preachers, teachers, students, church members, and anyone who wants to improve his or her understanding of the Bible.

Spring 1990   Harold F. Guite
                                                       Ivor H. Jones

PREFACE

Without the help of several people the production of this commentary would have been a much more daunting task. Therefore I should like to thank the Principal and Officers of the Bristol Baptist College for allowing me to use the facilities available in the College. I am grateful to all those who helped with the typing from my often barely legible manuscript, especially the College Secretary, Mrs Pearl Woolnough who supervised the work as well as doing a large part of it, and her assistant Mrs Ena Cole. My thanks are due also to the editors of Epworth Press for inviting me to have a small share in this considerable project which they have undertaken and for their help and understanding. If this commentary proves useful to those who read it then some of the credit must go to all these; if not, then the responsibility is mine!

Harry Mowvley

ABBREVIATIONS

BJRL	*Bulletin of the John Rylands Library*, Manchester
ET	English translation
JSOT	*Journal for the Study of the Old Testament*, Sheffield
NEB	New English Bible, 1970
REB	Revised English Bible, 1989
RSV	Revised Standard Version of the Bible, 1952
SOTS	Society for Old Testament Study

GENERAL INTRODUCTION

'Prophecy', as the word is used today, may be understood in at least three ways. First, it may refer simply to the prediction of future events. Those who apply it to the Old Testament in this way regard prophets like Amos and Hosea as foretellers of the future, and not just the imminent future but more distant events associated with the coming of Jesus. The prophetic books are then combed through to find any verses which may anticipate this event. These are few and far between in Amos and Hosea. For the most part these books are concerned with contemporary affairs, with God's attitude towards them and with the judgment he will bring on Israel for its part in them. Therefore they have to be seen in the first place as words dealing with events in the eighth century BCE.

Second, prophecy is sometimes spoken of as a gift of the Holy Spirit on the basis of I Cor. 12. Here it has relevance to the immediate contemporary situation and is meant to teach or warn Christians. Often it is regarded as a word from God which bears little if any relation to the speaker's own perception of events. It comes out of the blue as a word wholly from outside a person. There is no doubt that Amos and Hosea believed they were delivering a message from God, though by and large it was a word of threat rather than teaching or warning. Although it came out of the blue to them they often clothed it with observations of their own, made on the basis of what they had seen and understood. Moreover, nowhere do they attribute this to the spirit of God, nor do they give us any clear picture of the precise circumstances in which they received the message, or of the manner in which they heard it from God.

Third, we sometimes speak of prophetic preaching or of the prophetic task of the church. For some this means condemning injustice in every form both by individuals and by one part of society upon another. Injustice may then be defined as behaviour which infringes the rights of others as human beings. So imprisonment for conscience' sake, oppression of the poor, deprivation of racial minorities, discrimination on grounds of sex and colour all become legitimate topics of prophetic preaching. There is no denying that Amos in particular had much to say about the social evils of his day but he never falls into the trap of basing his criticism on some human principles of justice or rights and he never encourages the poor and oppressed to fight for their rights. As we shall discover this would be to turn his understanding of the word 'right' upside down. On the contrary he calls on those who are powerful to do what is right in society and threatens them for failure to do so. He bases this firmly on God's own 'right' activity towards Israel and on their relationship with him who brought them out of Egypt and into the Promised Land. So the criterion by which Amos judges the people is always the activity of God on their behalf and not some vague abstract notion of justice.

None of these modern ways of understanding 'prophecy', then, does full justice to Old Testament prophets like Amos and Hosea. Indeed each in some way distorts their function. They were God's messengers who lived close enough to God to understand what he had done for Israel and what sort of response he demanded. In the light of their own observations and experiences they were able to discern the voice of God and grasp the message they were to convey to their hearers. More often than not it was a condemnation for failure truly to be God's people and of consequent judgment in the more or less immediate future. Just here and there in the books as we now have them there are glimmerings of hope for the future as well.

It is important to remember that although these prophets are sometimes, mistakenly, called 'writing prophets' they probably wrote little or nothing themselves. The books which we possess refer to them, at certain points, in the third person. They are therefore books containing some of their words collected by others. The prophets themselves were above all speakers and the very language they used often displays oratorical rather than literary skills. Undoubtedly what they said was written down later by others and there is a time-lag between the speaking of God's word and the incorporation of that word into a book of sayings. How long this time gap was and what happened during it we can only surmise but there certain clues to help us. For instance, although both Amos and Hosea addressed the Northern Kingdom of Israel the books contain certain references to the Southern Kingdom of Judah. It is, of course, possible that occasionally they turned their eyes towards Judah and spoke to the people there, but several of such passages do seem out of place. No sweeping judgments can be made about this and each reference to Judah has to be examined in its context. There is a growing recognition that the words which Amos and Hosea used in Israel were carried south to Judah when Israel was conquered by the Assyrians and ceased to exist as a separate nation in 722 BCE. There in Judah their words were perceived to be still relevant and so could be re-used to threaten Judah. Sometimes this required a slight modification of their words to bring out their relevance. Then, when the books began to be compiled these new interpretations were included. The same process of reinterpretation probably continued beyond the fall of Jerusalem in 587 BCE and into the period of the exile in Babylon. What we now possess, therefore, are not only the original words of the prophets to Israel in the eighth century BCE, but some evidence of the way their words were preserved, reinterpreted and re-used in different circumstances simply because they were seen to be God's word.

Once this is realized it reminds us that the process of interpretation and preaching in which we are now engaged has a very long history. Lest we be tempted, however, to make the prophets' words mean whatever we want them to mean in our situation we have to listen carefully to what they meant in the circumstances in which they were first spoken, to consider what they meant to those who preserved them and used them in later generations. Then we may consider how they may be applied to our own situation today. The purpose of this commentary is to help readers to do just that.

BIBLIOGRAPHY

General

E. W. Heaton, *The Old Testament Prophets*, rev. ed., Darton, Longman & Todd and John Knox Press 1977

G. von Rad, *The Message of the Prophets*, ET SCM Press 1968, Harper & Row 1972

J. Lindblom, *Prophecy in Ancient Israel*, ET Blackwell 1973

R. E. Clements, *Prophecy and Tradition*, Blackwell and John Knox Press 1975

B. W. Anderson, *The Eighth Century Prophets*, Fortress Press and SPCK 1978

H. Mowvley, *Guide to Old Testament Prophecy*, Lutterworth 1979

J. Blenkinsopp, *A History of Prophecy in Israel*, SPCK and Westminster Press 1983

Amos

J. L. Mays, *Amos* (Old Testament Library), SCM Press and Westminster Press 1969

H. McKeating, *Amos, Hosea, Micah*, Cambridge University Press 1971

H. W. Wolff, *Joel and Amos* (Hermeneia), ET Fortress Press 1975

A. G. Auld, *Amos* (Old Testament Guides), JSOT Press 1986

J. A. Soggin, *The Prophet Amos*, SCM Press 1987

J. G. Hayes, *Amos, the Eighth-century Prophet: His Times and his Preaching*, Abingdon Press 1988

M. G. Polley, *Amos and the Davidic Empire*, Oxford University Press 1989

Hosea

N. Snaith, *Mercy and Sacrifice*, SCM Press 1953

J. L. Mays, *Hosea* (Old Testament Library), SCM Press and Westminster Press 1969

H. W. Wolff, *Hosea* (Hermeneia), ET Fortress Press 1974

G. I. Emmerson, *Hosea, an Israelite Prophet in Judaean Perspective*, JSOT Supplement Series 28, 1984

AMOS

Introduction

Prophecy in Israel

Amos was the first of Israel's prophets to have his words preserved in a book, but he was by no means the first prophet. Before him there had been other individuals such as Elijah, Elisha and Micaiah. There were also groups of prophets associated with them (I Kings 18. 1ff.; 22. 6ff.; II Kings 2. 3ff.; 4. 38ff.). Prior to that we read of a 'company of prophets coming down from the shrine' (I Sam. 10. 5ff.) and of Saul being 'filled with prophetic rapture'. David was advised by the prophet Nathan (II Samuel 12). Then there were 'seers' or 'men of God,' some of whom were expected to demand a fee for the information they could give (I Sam 9. 3ff.). Later on in the book of Deuteronomy Moses himself was called a prophet (Deut. 18. 15ff.).

Other nations, too, had their counterparts. At Mari in Mesopotamia, roughly a thousand years before Amos, there were people who, like Nathan, delivered messages from their god to the king.[1] In the Old Testament itself we read of the four hundred and fifty prophets of Baal and four hundred prophets of Asherah who had gone into Israel with Jezebel, the Tyrian princess who had become Ahab's wife (I Kings 18, 19).

There was, therefore, a considerable diversity of people to whom the description 'prophet' could be applied (cf. I Sam. 9. 9) and prophets remained active in the royal court down to the fall of Jerusalem in 587 BCE, sometimes in opposition to the so-called 'classical' prophets whose words appear in our Old Testament books (cf. Jeremiah and Hananiah in Jer. 27–28).

All this makes it very difficult to trace a history of prophecy in any

---

[1] For further details see H. Mowvley, *A Guide to Old Testament Prophecy*, pp. 5–8.

detail.[2] The nearest ancestors of Amos and Hosea were prophets like Elijah, Elisha and Micaiah who emerged from their groups with distinctive messages of their own which they firmly believed they had been commissioned by God to proclaim.

Amos

It was about the middle of the eighth century BCE that Amos began his prophetic task. We know nothing about him except what can be gained from the nine chapters of the book that bears his name, and that is not much. He is never mentioned in the 'historical' books of Kings and Chronicles. His home was somewhere near Tekoa in the Southern Kingdom of Judah although his prophetic activity took place in the Northern Kingdom of Israel. He had something to do with sheep and fig-trees (see commentary). He apparently had visions and was involved in a confrontation with the priest at Bethel (ch. 7).

Historical background

It would help us in our interpretation of his message if we knew more about him and about the circumstances in Israel when he prophesied there, but we have all too little information about either. To illustrate the difficulty, imagine a historian in 3000 CE coming across the words 'Never has so much been owed by so many to so few' without any accompanying information about the Battle of Britain and very little about the Second World War. In the absence of hard information he might well be tempted to argue that the vast expansion of credit in the 1980s, the aggressive advertising of loans and the huge national debts owed by some countries, of which he has evidence, had already begun in the 1940s and that therefore Winston Churchill's words were a description and criticism of the credit boom in its initial stages.

---

[2] The most recent attempt is J. Blenkinsopp, *A History of Prophecy in Israel*.

Needless to say he would be quite wrong, but who could blame him? Further, he might think to himself that the sentence was so carefully and cleverly constructed that it must have been worked over several times so as to become almost proverbial. However, if he knew more about Winston Churchill, he would realize that he was a man with a gift of oratory who could produce from his own mind such a striking sentence to meet the needs of the hour. Without information about Amos and his times it would be all too easy to make similar mistakes. Yet, as we have seen, we know little about Amos and we are not much better informed about his times.

The first verse of the book tells us that he began to prophesy in the 'days of Jeroboam, king of Israel'. That would be Jeroboam II. II Kings 14.23 says that he reigned for 41 years and this has been thought to cover the period c. 780–740 BCE, though some modern historians place his death about ten years earlier. Now we have a reasonable amount of information both from the Old Testament and from external sources about the preceding and following centuries but very little about those forty years or so. II Kings 14.25 says that Jeroboam restored Israel's borders 'from Lebo-hamath to the sea of the Arabah', that is, probably from the southern end of the Beqa'a valley to the Dead Sea. Two verses later we read that he 'recovered Damascus and Hamath'. There is also a mention of Jeroboam in I Chron. 5.11–22, where it is recorded that registers compiled in his day indicated that Israel and Judah together controlled central Transjordania. Some scholars think this represents the Chronicler's contemporary situation even though he intends us to understand that the information concerned a much earlier period. Neither Kings nor Chronicles has much interest in the Northern Kingdom except to condemn its kings. So the most we can say is that at some time in his reign Jeroboam undertook some successful campaigns to extend his sphere of influence.

When we look for external evidence in the records of surrounding nations we discover that Jeroboam is not mentioned in Assyrian documents of the period. This is probably because the Assyrians who had been active in the area previously were now preoccupied with internal problems and with attacks on their northern borders from some people called the Urartu.

Archaeology may perhaps throw some light on the situation. There is evidence of an earthquake around the middle of the eighth century BCE (Amos 1.1) though we cannot determine the precise date.

Excavations at Samaria over many years have revealed some 500 pieces of ivory from panels or inlays, some of them depicting gods of Egypt and Assyria (Amos 3.15). Much of this material originated in the days of Omri and Ahab a century earlier (I Kings 22.39) but was still around in the days of Jeroboam. We cannot say whether the depictions of foreign gods on the ivories mean that those gods were worshipped in Samaria or whether the pieces had simply come to be there in the course of trade with those countries. From the same period down to the reign of Jeroboam come pieces of pottery (ostraka) on which were inscribed details of payments of oil and wine with the names of those making and receiving payments. Since they were found in royal quarters they probably represent payments made from vineyards which were owned by the king but let out to tenants. Many of the names of people from the country districts have 'baal' as a component while those closer to or within the city are compounded with YHWH or YH. This could indicate that Baal was worshipped in the country districts. On the other hand 'baal' may simply have been understood as a title for YHWH meaning 'lord'. What these payments say about Israel's social structure archaeology itself cannot tell us. We have to interpret the evidence with the help of what we can find elsewhere.

Of Bethel, where Amos seems to have been particularly active, archaeology offers us little information for this period. Neither the golden bull which is said to have been installed there by Jeroboam I, nor the sanctuary in which it stood have been found. There is evidence of Bethel's destruction in 722 BCE.

The point of all this is to emphasize how little we know about the years 780–740 BCE. It means that we have to rely on what we find in the book of Amos itself, but we have seen how easy it is to misinterpret sayings when we do not know the situation to which they were addressed.

The prevailing view about the background to Amos is that he was at work in a time of comparative peace and prosperity. This is based on the belief that, when Assyria was more concerned with domestic affairs, Israel was free to develop her own economy without interference. During the eighth century, therefore, the rich became richer and the poor peasants became poorer. The message of Amos is then interpreted as an attack on the wealthy for their greed, their lack of concern and justice for the poor and for their elaborate worship, which became more important to them than God himself. Much of this tends to be based on a circular argument. We discover the social background to Amos by interpreting his words and then interpret his words against that background.

Recently, however, other suggestions have been made. Max Polley[3] has suggested that Amos was a strongly nationalistic Judaean prophet who believed that the Davidic Empire represented the true destiny of Israel. The nations mentioned in Amos 1 and 2 were criticized because they had rebelled against the Davidic rule and had broken free. Israel too had broken away when Jeroboam I established a separate nation of Israel with its own king and shrine in 922 BCE. The shrines at Bethel and elsewhere, as well as the Northern monarchy, were therefore schismatic and sinful in Amos' view. His preaching in Israel was a call to Israel to return to the fold by rejoining Judah under its king of the Davidic line. Since they refused, Israel, like the rest of the nations, would be severely punished but eventually the new Davidic Kingdom would be established. This allows him to interpret certain passages in a new but consistent way. If we knew that Amos was such a prophet it would help us to understand his words but we do not. We can only surmise that he was by interpreting his words in a certain way.

J. H. Hayes[4] has a different view of the fortunes of Israel. From careful examination of Assyrian records and Old Testament texts he reaches the conclusion that up to about 800 BCE Israel was strong only when Assyria was strong and active in the area. Generally Israel's rulers were pro-Assyrian. When Assyria's influence was removed, however, the anti-Assyrian nations like Damascus became a threat to Israel. So, in the eighth century, towards the end of Jeroboam's reign, Israel was severely threatened. Moreover he believes that there was an anti-Assyrian faction within Israel in that same period led by Pekah, who eventually became king. Meanwhile Judah throughout the period was subject to Israel. Far from being a time of peace, then, the time of Amos was one of near civil war and his words can be interpreted in the light of Pekah's threat to Jeroboam from the territory which he controlled in Transjordania and his coronation as a rival king to Jeroboam in the year 750/749 BCE. Again, if this historical scenario were correct it would give us a different perception of Amos' message. Much of it, though, is derived from a new interpretation of

[3] M. G. Polley, *Amos and the Davidic Empire*.
[4] J. H. Hayes, *Amos: his Times and his Preaching*.

the evidence we have concerning the century or so prior to Jeroboam II and we have seen that this is not a safe way of interpreting his words.

Both these recent studies make interesting suggestions which have to be taken into account as we proceed. It remains true, however, that each interpretation of Amos, including this present one, is based on limited information about him and about the situation he addressed. Much of this depends upon the interpretation itself, but until fresh evidence comes to light from elsewhere, if ever it does, we have no alternative but to proceed in this way. Here the more conventional view is followed that times were fairly peaceful and relatively prosperous when Amos preached and that the Assyrian threat was still far enough away in the future to have no influence upon his message of judgment which is couched in general terms and not in terms of attack by Assyria.[5]

[5] Since this book was written, another interpretation has been suggested by Stanley N. Roseenbaum, *Amos of Israel*, Mercer University Press 1990. He sees Amos as an Israelite civil servant who because of his outspoken criticism of his government was exiled to Judah on grounds of treason and settled in Tekoa.

Commentary

Introductory verse

1.1 The person or persons who put together the prophecies of Amos into a book placed this verse here to provide us with some information about Amos himself and the times in which he proclaimed to the people the word of God. The information about the prophet is meagre indeed. We should like to know a good deal more about him but the compiler was much more interested in what Amos said than who he was. This lack of detail about the prophet's background and life is not confined to Amos. The same applies to most of the prophets and even when we think we know more about some of them, such as Hosea and Jeremiah, closer study shows that the interest of the compilers is not in the person but in the message. Details of their lives therefore are included only in so far as they contribute to the message they are to proclaim.

Of Amos we are not told anything at all about his family background, not even his father's name. We are told that he was *one of the sheep-farmers of Tekoa* presumably because it was important for the reader to know this. The word translated sheep-farmer occurs in only one other place in the Old Testament, in II Kings 3.4 where it is used to describe the activity of King Mesha of Moab and where REB translates it as 'sheep-breeder'. A similar word is used in certain writings discovered at Ugarit in Northern Syria. These are written in a Canaanite language to which Hebrew bears some resemblance. There it is used in a passage which speaks of priests. Exactly what we are to make of this is not clear. Some have thought it leads to the conclusion that Amos, too, had links with cultic personnel or raised sheep specially for sacrifice. What we can say with a fair degree of certainty from these two passages is that Amos was not, as was once thought, a simple shepherd looking after someone else's sheep on the barren area around Tekoa and therefore uneducated and unaware of what was going on in the world at large. Indeed his words also reveal a considerable grasp of both social and international affairs. Later in the book, in ch. 7.15, Amos himself is quoted as saying that he *followed the flock*, which suggests that he did some actual shepherding, but also that he was a *herdsman*, a word more commonly used with reference to cattle but perhaps used here inclusively of sheep as well, and a *fig-grower*. Again we are uncertain about the precise meaning of this latter term. It has been suggested that it refers to the job of opening newly formed figs in order to let out the grubs, so enabling the figs to ripen without hindrance. On the other hand the figs may have been grown as food for the sheep as a kind of supplementary occupation. So although Amos may sometimes have *followed the flock* we should see him primarily as a sheep farmer breeding sheep and growing figs on his farm.

His home was in *Tekoa*. This was a town some 16 kilometres south of Jerusalem. The significance of this is that it was in the Kingdom of Judah and not in the Northern Kingdom of Israel, to which Amos was to address his prophecies. As far as the people of Israel was concerned he was an outsider, not exactly a foreigner, because both kingdoms recognized a common origin and worshipped the same God, but an outsider, because each nation had its own monarchy and its own religious shrines and institutions. Indeed from time to time there were hostilities between them. Although we ought not to make too much of this fact, it should be borne in mind throughout, for it does call into question Amos' authority as a prophet to Israel (see 7.12ff.). *Tekoa* was not exactly a backwater. It had been fortified by Rehoboam, Solomon's son, after the division of the old Davidic Kingdom in 922 BCE (II Chron. 11.6), and it was a store city with its own governor. It is also mentioned in II Sam. 14.2 as the home of an unnamed wise woman who was called in by Joab to try to persuade David to get rid of his favourite but dangerous son Absalom. It has been suggested that such a 'wisdom school' or 'circle' continued to the time of Amos and his contact with it accounts for certain elements of style and content which bear resemblance to the wisdom traditions as found, say, in the book of Proverbs (see on 3.3–8). Again it would be wrong to build too much on such slight evidence. Educated people generally were probably familiar with so-called 'wisdom' teaching and, as we have seen, Amos was probably a man of substance and well educated.

The other thing we are told about Amos is that *he received* his *words in visions*. Now it is true that Amos is said to have seen visions – five of them are mentioned in chs. 7, 8 and 9. It would be wrong to assume that this was the only way in which he received his message from God. Indeed again and again he is said to pass on *words*. In fact in this present passage the Hebrew may be translated literally 'the words . . . which Amos saw' and the word 'saw' is sometimes used of seeing visions (Ezek. 12.27), but may also mean 'to see' in the sense of understand (Job 27.12), as in our phrase 'Do you see?'. In Amos 7.12 Amaziah uses the participle of the same verb as a noun to describe Amos as a *seer* and, as we shall see, that is a term which is said to have become synonymous with 'prophet' (I Sam. 9.9). We should therefore not press this statement about Amos too hard. It is used to indicate that Amos received his message in a special way by revelation and not through the literal speech of God.

The introductory verse then tells in whose reign Amos was active. *Uzziah king of Judah* (c. 768–740 BCE) *and Jeroboam son of Jehoash king of Israel* (793–752 BCE). The order in which they are mentioned almost certainly indicates the Judaean perspective from which the book was finally put together. Since both kings reigned for a long time according to the book of Kings, the note does not allow us to place Amos' prophecies too precisely. It is usually held that these long reigns indicate stability in both kingdoms and comparative peace and prosperity (see Introduction). The rise of Tiglath Pileser as king of Assyria (c. 745 BCE) and his aim to expand his territory westwards towards the Mediterranean changed this situation, and in some twelve years Damascus was captured (732 BCE) and much of Israel's territory annexed. In another ten years Samaria fell after a lengthy siege (722 BCE). The prophecies of Amos make no mention of any of these events and, though he can describe Israel's coming downfall in military terms, he never mentioned Assyria as the agent of it. It is therefore usual to place Amos' activity sometime between 760 and 750 BCE. Partly because he assesses the political situation differently J. H. Hayes places his prophecies much more precisely as being proclaimed just prior to the autumnal Feast of Tabernacles in 750/749 BCE.[1] It is doubtful whether we can be so precise.

The final statement in v. 1, *two years before the earthquake*, seems to give greater precision, but, in fact, although there is archaeological

---

[1] Hayes, *Amos*, p. 38.

evidence of an earthquake within these ten years, we cannot say exactly when it occurred. On several sites such as Hazor in the north there was considerable destruction in this period and, since stones toppled in all directions, this is usually attributed to the earthquake. Curiously though this event is hardly ever mentioned explicitly in the Old Testament. The only other text where it occurs is in the latest part of Zechariah (14.5). There the prophet anticipates a day when the mountain on which Jerusalem stands will be split in two and the valley formed between the two halves blocked 'as it was in the time of King Uzziah of Judah'. We are bound to ask, therefore, why the editor of Amos chooses to mention it here. If it had been just to fix the date of Amos more precisely it would have been easy enough to say in what year of Uzziah's or Jeroboam's reign Amos was preaching. There is probably some other significance in it. Perhaps it seemed to be the partial fulfilment of Amos' threats in e.g. 5.16; 8.8; 9.1. Perhaps it was because the appearing of YHWH was often depicted by an earthquake (cf Ex. 19.17f.; I Kings 19.14; Ps. 18.7ff.) and Amos had spoken of the day of YHWH and the fact that Israel must meet him (e.g. 4.12).

As far as we can tell Amos does not seem to have been a lifelong prophet like Isaiah and Jeremiah. Rather he was taken from his sheep-farm in Tekoa, sent to Samaria and Bethel in Israel to proclaim God's word, after which he presumably returned to Tekoa; presumably, because we do not actually know. We are not told.

Summary introduction

1.2 This historical introduction over, the editor next gives us a verse from Amos which will act as a summary introduction of his message before proceeding to the long series of sayings about Israel and its neighbours. The verse is important for two reasons. First, it introduces us to the prophetic style of speaking, which was a loosely poetic form of speech. The English translation in REB catches something of the rhythmic nature of it though it is even more marked in the Hebrew where each line has three stressed syllables.

> *The LORD roars from Zion*
> *and utters his voice from Jerusalem;*

the shepherds' pastures are dried up
and the choicest farmland is parched.

Rarely does the Hebrew poetry have rhyme, but this rhythm is important. Although this particular verse may have been polished, it was perfectly possible even in impromptu speech to maintain a rhythmic form. Another characteristic of Hebrew poetry is its 'parallelism'. This may take a number of different forms. In this verse the first and third lines are echoed in the second and fourth by use of synonyms or associated words. *Roars* is parallel with *thunders* (or 'utters his voice'). *Zion* is parallel with *Jerusalem*. *The shepherds' pastures* and *the choicest farmland* correspond, as do *dried up* and *parched*. A recognition of this is important, because sometimes a 'parallel' word can throw light on the meaning of an otherwise obscure word. The purpose of parallelism is not mere repetition but to provide a slightly different perspective, and the two lines taken together have greater effect than one single line would have. Doubtless also it would help people to remember what had been said.

Second, and even more important, is the content of the verse, for it threatens a word from YHWH which sounds like a lion's roar and it is a word of devastation. The verb 'to roar' is used of a lion in Judg. 14.5; Amos 3.4, 5; Ps. 104.21 and YHWH's voice is often used to denote thunder (cf. Ps. 29). Amos' message, therefore, is as terrifying as a lion about to pounce on its prey or as the thunder pealing from heaven. The reference to the *shepherds' pastures* and *choicest farmland* was appropriate enough for Amos. For these to dry up would be a disaster not only for people like himself but for the whole nation. Yet this is the 'motto' for all his preaching. One rather curious feature of the verse is the reference to *Zion* and *Jerusalem* in a message which was intended not for Judah but for Israel. It is true that this may well have reflected Amos's own belief, for as a Judaean he would have doubtless agreed with Isa. 2.3 and Micah 4.2 that 'the word of the LORD comes from Jerusalem'. Whilst by no means the only shrine, Jerusalem, ever since the time of David, had been the place where people might expect to meet with God and hear his word. If, however, Amos had said this at Bethel, where he did much of his preaching, he certainly would not have won the support of his hearers who would have resented the assumption that YHWH did not address his people also at Bethel, Jacob's shrine. Some commentators therefore either regard the whole verse as a Judaean composition by the editor to provide a 'theme' for Amos' preaching or suggest that *Zion* and *Jerusalem* have been substituted for an original Bethel. The fact is, of course, that since the verse stands entirely on its own we cannot know the circumstances in which it was first spoken. It may not have been Amos' opening word at Bethel; it could have come from a later period, especially when we remind ourselves that in 7.12–16 Amos was told to do his prophesying in Judah. Whatever conclusion we may come to about its authenticity, it sums up Amos' message admirably and provides the key signature for the whole composition.[2]

[2] Polley, *Amos*, pp. 109f., regards the verse as from Amos and as part of his polemic against the Northern shrines.

The sins of Israel and her neighbours
Amos 1.3–2.16

This long section of the book is presented as a well-rounded whole. Seven foreign, neighbouring nations are condemned for various crimes and threatened with judgment, leading up to a similar condemnation of Israel itself. They were all smaller nations at present independent of the two major powers of Assyria and Egypt. All eight oracles follow a similar though not identical pattern, the final one against Israel being considerably extended. If we can imagine Amos pronouncing these oracles, then the intention clearly seems to be to win the approval of Israel for the condemnation of the foreigners and then to turn the same searchlight of disapproval and threat upon Israel itself. The whole series makes the attack on Israel more telling and startling.

Each member of the series begins in the same way, *For crime after crime* . . . but this translation, though adequate, obscures the fact that they are all introduced by 'numerical sayings' which appear to have been used for teaching especially in Wisdom circles. Earlier translations such as RSV bring this out more clearly. 'For three crimes of. . . . yes, for four . . .' would be a more literal translation. In this form of teaching usually the second and higher number indicates the number of items to be spelled out (cf. Prov. 30. 15ff.). Here, however, this is not adhered to strictly. Sometimes only one, sometimes more than one *crime* is mentioned. So far as the passage about Israel is concerned it is possible to discern four crimes but a different division of the verses could disclose seven! It does not seem as though the number has any special significance. The word translated *crime* often refers to political acts of rebellion. Polley[1] takes this to mean rebellion from the Davidic Empire and argues that all seven nations were guilty of this and that Amos condemned Israel for the same reason. In 922

[1] *Amos*, pp. 66ff.

15

BCE they had seceded from the Kingdom of David. Usually, however, the word is thought to refer to rebellion against YHWH's kingship even though the other nations may not recognize his authority.

Closer examination of the first seven sayings reveals certain differences and some repetition. The sayings against Tyre (vv. 9–10), Edom (vv. 11–12) and Judah (2.4–5) all lack the concluding formula *It is the word of the LORD*. All seven nations are threatened with fire but apart from these same three the threat is amplified in various ways, chiefly by including the ruler in the threat. Both Gaza and Tyre are accused of deporting *a whole community to Edom*. Finally Judah's crimes are different in character from the rest in that they are religious not international crimes. These facts inevitably throw some doubt on the authenticity of some of the seven passages. Seven may be thought to be an appropriate number, but, if the three mentioned above are omitted, we are left with four which is just as appropriate a number! There are other factors, too, which will be dealt with when we look at each in turn which strongly suggest that the oracles against *Damascus, Gaza, the Ammonites* and *Moab* were spoken by Amos while the remaining three were added by Judaean preachers at a later date and so became included in the final edition of the book.

It might be easier to come to a decision about this if we could identify the incidents which are described in each section, but this, too, is difficult. For Amos' strategy to have maximum impact his hearers would have to be fully aware of the actions of one nation against another and that may suggest that they were all of recent occurrence. Unfortunately, relations between these smaller nations in the middle of the eighth century are not well documented either in the Old Testament or elsewhere. As we shall see when we examine each individual oracle in more detail there are several possibilities ranging from recent animosity[2] to ancient antagonism. In any case there is much to be said for the view of John Barton[3] that in the ancient world there were certain generally accepted conventions or understandings governing the conduct of war and that these actions, whenever they took place, were violations of them. Such conventions are not dependent on common religious convictions; they simply indicate that there are certain kinds of action which human beings

---

[2] Hayes, *Amos*, of course sees these crimes as perpetated during the period of near civil war towards the end of the reign of Jeroboam.

[3] John Barton, *Amos's Oracles against the Nations* (SOTS Monograph series 6), Cambridge University Press 1980.

ought not to perform against each other. We may be reminded here of Paul's argument in Rom. 2. 12ff. that 'when Gentiles who do not possess the law carry out its precepts by the light of nature, then, although they have no law, they are their own law.'

There are three other things to be said about these oracles against the nations which give some insight into Amos' beliefs. First, not all the crimes are committed against Israel. It is not clear at all who is meant by the *whole community* in vv. 6 and 9. It may be Israel or part of Israel but it could equally well refer to some other group. More particularly Moab's crime in 2.1–3 is certainly not against Israel but against Edom. We cannot say, therefore, that Amos was venting his own anger or playing on the feelings of the Israelites by condemning Israel's enemies for attacks made on Israel. It would also be going too far to claim that Amos was a strict monotheist who believed that one God governed the affairs of all nations, whoever they were and whatever God they worshipped. This leads on to the second point. In each case the *crime* committed evokes the anger and the judgment of YHWH. Though they may not recognize YHWH's authority over them, the nations are held responsible for their own conduct and, if they go beyond what is generally acceptable, then they will be punished and, as far as Amos is concerned, the punishment will be carried out by YHWH. He thus shares with Isaiah the belief in YHWH's ultimate authority over other nations (cf. Isa. 10.5ff., where the Assyrians are 'the rod I wield in my anger'; and when the king of Assyria puts his victory down to his own power then YHWH will in time punish him). Third, and we shall return to this later, what is so startling and certainly would have been to the Israelites is that the social evils which are to be found within Israel are just as serious in YHWH's eyes as the international crimes committed by other nations. Crimes against the poor and underprivileged were seen as being every bit as offensive to YHWH as the national offences against human decency. It is still difficult for us to come to terms with such a view, for we prefer to differentiate between one type of offence and another according to their seriousness.

Against Damascus

1.3–6   The opening formula *These are the words of the LORD* introduces each of the eight oracles. More familiar in the form 'Thus saith the LORD', this has become known as the 'messenger formula' since it was the conventional way in which a messenger began the message he was charged to deliver. We should not necessarily think that the message had been learned by heart to be delivered verbatim. Quite probably the messenger passed on the message in his own words. Although the phrase is most commonly found as an introduction to a prophetic speech it is found also in secular contexts, where it probably originated (cf. Gen.32. 4ff. where the same Hebrew phrase is found 'Thus said Jacob your servant'). It therefore tells us something about the relationship between God and his prophet. The latter is YHWH's messenger charged to deliver a message he has received from YHWH to the people concerned. It does not imply that the words the prophet used were put directly on his lips by YHWH. Rather it underlines the fact that when he speaks his message the prophet does so with the authority of God. At the same time he does not use indirect speech ('YHWH said that he . . .') but direct ('I will . . .') for he speaks in the name of YHWH.

THE WORD OF THE LORD

The Old Testament speaks frequently about the 'word of the LORD' and in view of the common use of the 'messenger formula' by the prophets in which they pass on the 'word of the LORD' we need to grasp the significance and importance of it as early as possible. In Hebrew the equivalent of 'word' is *dābār*, but this word may also be translated as 'thing' or 'matter', particularly in the phrase 'after these things'. While etymological considerations must not be given too much weight, there is obviously some connection between a word spoken and a thing done. It is a well-known fact that in the creation narrative in Genesis 1 God has only to speak and things come into being. Such a view of the power of the spoken word is not confined to Israel. In Babylonian mythology the god Marduk may bring a garment into being by means of a spoken word and destroy it by means of another. Ps. 33.6 makes the same point about the creation of the heavens: 'The word of the LORD created the heavens; all the host of heaven was formed at his command.'

A word, then, and especially the 'word of the LORD', carried with it considerable authority and power, power to accomplish what it said. Once it had been spoken it was as though the very 'word' became objectified and took on a life of its own as it moved towards its fulfilment (cf. Isa. 55.10ff.).

So by reporting and speaking the 'word of the LORD' the prophet is not merely describing what the LORD has said by way of threat or promise. He is nudging the word forward towards its fulfilment and his reporting of the message becomes part of the process. This is why prophets generally were treated with respect. They could also sometimes be put to death because their threatening words were seen as a real threat. It was therefore important to know whether a prophet's words really were the 'word of the LORD', as they claimed by using the formula, or whether they were simply an expression of their own minds. It was not easy to discern the true from the false prophet, and the matter is dealt with for instance in Deut. 18.20,21f. and more fully in the narrative of Jeremiah and Hananiah in Jer. 27 and 28.

Sometimes the prophet did speak his own words, especially when he was describing the situation he was about to condemn, but then usually he would inject a 'word of YHWH' introduced by the 'messenger formula' or by an oath (cf. Amos 4.1, 2–3). If, then, Amos really was a prophet, a messenger of God, his words were highly dangerous and seditious (cf. 7.12).

In the prologue to John's Gospel the 'word' was not only involved in creation, or passed on by prophets. It had become embodied in a person, Jesus, whose life says to us all that God has to say to human-kind.

This view of the word is not to be confused with a magical spell. The 'word of the LORD' possessed its power only as an expression of YHWH's own power and will and was always under his ultimate control. He, and he alone, could revoke it, call it back, stay its fulfilment, as is suggested by 1.3.

Damascus was the capital of Syria and was often used to designate the country and not just the city. It was situated to the north-west of Israel and was an important trading centre between Egypt and Assyria. When relatively free from interference from either of these two greater powers Syria always presented a threat to Israel. They had been allied with the Ammonites in the war against David (II Sam. 10, where they are called Aramaeans). In the middle of the ninth century Ben-hadad was king and Elijah was commissioned to replace him with Hazael (I Kings 19.15). Later there were several skirmishes between Syria and Israel (II Kings 5.1f.) and Ben-hadad besieged Samaria (II Kings 6.24ff.). Elisha fulfilled the commission given to Elijah by encouraging Hazael to assassinate Ben-hadad (II Kings 8). The fact that *Hazael* and *Ben-hadad* are both mentioned in v. 4 may indicate that the Syrian dynasty still went by these names, unless indeed Amos was referring to the events which had taken place a century earlier.

I shall grant them no reprieve is a perfectly good modern translation of the Hebrew but it does obscure a certain ambiguity. A more literal translation would be 'I will not cause it to return' and the ambiguity lies in the 'it', for it is not clear what it referred to. As it now stands it seems to refer back to the lion's roar in v. 2. But if we are right in thinking that v. 2 was originally a quite separate saying from vv. 3ff. then 'it' had no antecedent and we should probably assume that it is either the word of God or the punishment which is about to be threatened. Admittedly in the long run it makes little difference, for the roar of the lion, the word of God and the threatened punishment all amount to the same thing, the destruction of *Damascus* and the *exile* of its *people*.

The *crime* consists of a brutal attack on *Gilead* which lay east of the Jordan on the southern border of Syria. The nearest reference to any such attack in the Old Testament is in II Kings 10.32ff., where we are told that Hazael the ruler of Syria sought to recapture Transjordanian territory, including Gilead, during the reign of Jehu who, also at Elijah's instigation, overthrew Ahab and liquidated all his family, an event mentioned also in Hosea 1. 4. This may help to account for the use of *Hazael* and *Ben-hadad* to denote the Syrian royal house. According to II Kings 14. 25, 28, Jeroboam II recaptured Damascus from the Syrians and presumably repossessed Gilead.

Amos' description of the Syrian attack on Gilead is almost certainly metaphorical. By dragging a flat piece of wood with iron nails driven through it over a heap of reaped corn a farmer would separate the grain from the chaff. What the Syrians actually did cannot, of course, be known but presumably it was something brutal to warrant the use of such a metaphor.

In all seven oracles the punishment begins with a reference to *fire*. In this instance it is filled out by a threat of destruction to the *nobles* and probably the king and a threat of exile to the people. *Those who live in the vale of Aven* is singular, not plural, in the Hebrew and more probably refers to 'him who sits (on the throne)'. The verb 'to sit' often bears this meaning. This makes the second line of v. 3 parallel with the third and not with the first. In fact the Hebrew word translated *nobles* in the first line is better rendered 'gate-bar' (see RSV), a wooden bar fitting in two slots to hold a door or gate firmly shut. Then the line would mean that *Damascus* would be open to any invader, who would carry off both ruler and people. *The vale of Aven* and *Beth-eden* cannot safely be identified. Since 'aven' represents the Hebrew for 'wickedness' or 'idolatry' and 'eden' represents the Hebrew for 'pleasure', it is possible that both are nicknames for Syrian towns. Hosea uses Beth-aven as a nickname for Bethel (10.5). *Kir* is also unidentified.

The oracle concludes with the formula *It is the word of the LORD* or, perhaps better, 'oracle of YHWH'.

Against Gaza

1.6–8 *Gaza* was one of the five Philistine cities on the coastal plain to the south-west of Judah. Although only one city is mentioned here it is virtually certain that the whole pentapolis is intended, since three of the remaining cities are threatened with punishment and the term *Philistines* covering all of them is used. The missing city is Gath, but we should not place too much weight on this, since nowhere in the Old Testament are all five cities mentioned together. In any case Gath is mentioned later in 6.2. The Philistines had given Israel a great deal of trouble in the early days of Saul and Samuel but they had been subdued by David and ceased to play any significant part in Israel's affairs, though they apparently were independent of Israel and Judah. *Gaza* was perhaps picked out as being a centre for slave trading, for this appears to be the *crime* of which the city was accused. The use of people taken captive in war as slaves was normal practice, and clearly something more than this is intended here. There are probably two things which make this into a *crime*. First, *they deported a whole community into exile*. Presumably they had been at war with someone and had carried off all the people. Who that *community* was we are not told, and there is nothing recorded in the Old Testament to allow us to guess. Without stronger evidence it is unsafe to assume that they were Israelites, though they may have been. II Chron. 21.16ff. does speak of an attack on Judah under King Joram by Philistines and others, and adds that 'they carried off all the property which they found in the king's palace, as well as his sons and wives; not a son was left to him except the youngest, Jehoahaz' (or Ahaziah). According to II Kings 9.27ff. Ahaziah was killed in Jehu's purge almost a century before Amos' time. While Chronicles says Joram was attacked by Philistines, II Kings 8.20ff. records a revolt of *Edom* against Judah as a result of which it gained its independence. We noted the possibility that the *crime of Damascus* may have taken place during Jehu's reign. It is just possible that the *crime* of the *Philistines* took place in the same period and the *whole community* was the Judaean royal household. Second, those taken captive were not used as slaves by their captors but were sold on *to Edom*. There is nothing to indicate why *Edom* should require a *whole community* as slaves, but if they had just gained independence from Judah they may have welcomed the opportunity to use Judaeans in this way.

The punishment threatened was virtually the same as in the case of Damascus. As in v. 5 the phrase *those who live in . . .* (v. 8) is a singular participle and more likely refers to 'him who sits (on the throne)' making a good parallel with *sceptred ruler*.

Against Tyre

1.9–10   *Tyre*, the chief city of Phoenicia, on the coast to the north-west of Israel, had strong ties with Israel. Solomon had hired workmen from *Tyre* when he was building the Temple complex in Jerusalem (I Kings 5). Later the Israelite prince Ahab was married to the Tyrian princess Jezebel, most probably to cement an agreement between the two countries, when Omri was building his new capital in Samaria (I Kings 16.23f.). She was killed in Jehu's purge, to which we have already referred (II Kings 9.36). If this is a genuine saying of Amos, then *ignoring the brotherly alliance* could have some reference to this agreement. We have no record, however, of a Phoenician attack on Israel at this time.

We have already seen that this is one of the seven oracles upon which doubt is cast because there is no expansion of the threat of *fire* and because the concluding formula *It is the word of the LORD* is missing. There are other reasons for doubt as well. First, the idea of 'remembering' or 'forgetting' (here *ignoring*) a *covenant* is found elsewhere only in the later priestly writings. Second, we are bound to ask why *Edom* should want another *whole community* as well as the one from Gaza.

The likelihood is that *Tyre* was included in the list at a later stage, but then we should need to ask why. Was it just to complete the circuit of smaller states surrounding Israel, or was there a time later when *Tyre* had broken faith with Judah? No such incident is recorded in the Old Testament, but among the oracles against foreign nations in Isa. 23; Ezek. 26; 27; 28 are found threats against Tyre which indicate that there had been great respect for the city before it overreached itself. Moreover in Jer. 25.22; 27.3, it is listed with Moab, Edom, and Ammon among others. Consequently there will have been good reason for a Judaean using Amos' oracles at a later date to include one about *Tyre*, which, like *Gaza*, had a reputation for slave trading (Ezek. 27.13; Joel 3.4–8).

It could be argued that anyone making such an addition would be careful to conform closely to Amos' style, but that would be to misunderstand the process. The later preachers and editors had no wish to delude their hearers or readers into thinking that these were Amos' words. They were content to show how his message was still relevant and could be applied to their situation.

Against Edom

1.11–12 This is another oracle over which hangs some doubt. *Edom* was situated to the south of Judah. According to tradition there were close ties between Israel (both Israel and Judah together) and Edom. The text here calls them *kinsmen*. The ancestors of Israel and Edom were Jacob and Esau, who were twin brothers (Gen. 25.19ff.). Esau was the elder but Jacob received Isaac's blessing by deceit (Gen. 27). The breach between them was healed somewhat at their later meeting (Gen. 32). *Stifling their natural affections* is an attempt to make sense of some difficult Hebrew which also is intended to describe the relationship. A more literal translation would be 'he was destroying (or, trying to destroy) his wombs'! The plural form 'wombs' may signify 'compassion' – hence, *natural affections* – but the verb 'destroy' suggests something less abstract. Some, therefore, prefer to render 'he tried to destroy his twin (womb-mate)', which would provide a good parallel with the following line. On the basis of other Ancient Near Eastern texts, others translate the term as 'maidens' (cf Judg. 5.30).

There is little evidence in the Old Testament for such an Edomite attack on the Northern state of Israel, though there was a dispute between Judah and Edom over possession of the port of Elath in the eighth century (II Kings 14.22) and it was recaptured by Edom in the reign of Ahaz (II Kings 16.6).

There was, however, a great deal of animosity during the Babylonian exile, when the Edomites took advantage of the absence of Judaean leaders to encroach upon its territory and even to advance into what had been Israel (cf. Ezek. 35 and Obad.). It would be entirely appropriate for a Judaean preacher to add Edom to the list of nations deserving to be destroyed by *fire*.

Teman denotes a district in the north of Edom, while *Bozrah* is a city fortified in the eighth century.

Against the Ammonites

1.13–15 The nation of Ammon is almost always referred to by the name of its people, the 'children of Ammon' or *Ammonites* as it is properly translated here. Their home was to the east of the Jordan, between Gilead in the north and Moab in the south. Traditionally they were the offspring of Lot's incest with his daughters (Gen. 19.30ff.). They attacked Jabesh-gilead and besieged it but Saul relieved the city and as a result was crowned Israel's first king (I Sam. 11). David was also engaged in war with them (II Sam. 8–12).

Their crime was that *they ripped open the pregnant women in Gilead* on account of *their greed for land*. In all probability we should not think of a single historical incident but of a more prolonged series of border skirmishes which were not likely to find their way into the historical records, and indeed there is no mention of this in Kings or Chronicles. We may perhaps assume that it had happened recently enough to be still fresh in the memory of Israelite people listening to Amos. More than this we cannot say.

The ripping open of *pregnant women* was not an ordinary act of warfare but a particularly fierce and cruel practice, generally outlawed by decent people. Elisha wept at the thought of Hazael becoming King of Syria because he believed that he would 'dash the children of the Israelites to the ground and rip open their pregnant women' (II Kings 8.12). It was practised by Menahem in the last days of Israel when he carried out his coup to become king (II Kings 15.16). Hosea threatens that it will be practised against Israel by an enemy, presumably Assyria (Hosea 13.16). The aim of the practice was probably to prevent the birth of potential enemies. In the course of border warfare this would make encroachment all the easier, not only in the present because of the ferocity of the act but also in the future since there would be less resistance.

The usual punishment by *fire* is promised (v. 14) and this is filled out by reference to *war* and *whirlwind* in the *day of battle* and *sweeping tempest*. Whether Amos had in mind future defeat by the Assyrians is uncertain. As we shall see he never mentioned Assyria as the means of punishment of Israel. It seems as though his certainty of coming judgment was due to his belief in the justice of God rather than to any awareness of impending attack and defeat. The words for 'whirlwind' and 'sweeping tempest' are used together as the instruments of YHWH's wrath in Ps. 83.15. This will involve the exile of *their king* and his court. The Hebrew of *their king* is *malkām* and the name of the Ammonite god was *Milkōm* according to I Kings 11.5. Perhaps Amos was making a deliberate play on words.

Rabbah, the modern Amman, was the capital of Ammon and the only Ammonite city mentioned in the Old Testament.

Against Moab

2.1–3 The land of *Moab* was situated to the south of Ammon and the east of the Dead Sea. Relations with Israel were rarely friendly. Numbers 25 records that the Israelites were led astray by Moabite women as they were about to enter the Promised Land and began to worship Moabite gods. Later Moab was subdued by David (II Sam. 8.2ff.) even though his line was eventually traced back to Ruth, a Moabitess (Ruth 4.17–22). Moab then rebelled under King Mesha in the reign of Ahab in the ninth century (II Kings 3.4ff.). However, the *crime* of which Amos accused the Moabites was not against Israel but against their southern neighbours, Edom. In the earlier oracles the victims were either unspecified or Israel. In this case only is it made clear that a crime committed by one foreign nation against another is also the concern of God and that a breach of the conventions of natural decent human and national relationships earns his punishment. As we have said already (p. 17) this should not be taken as evidence that Amos was a strict monotheist and universalist denying the existence of all other gods. Rather YHWH is the only god as far as he and Israel/Judah are concerned and he is just. Therefore he cannot tolerate injustice wherever it may be found. Philosophical or doctrinal questions about monotheism would not have made much sense to Amos.

The crime itself was that *they burnt to lime the bones of the king of Edom*. This was not simply a reference to cremation, though that was repugnant to the Israelites; it involved the desecration of the royal tombs in places like Petra, where many Edomite kings were buried in caves. The *bones* were *burnt to lime*, which according to Deut. 27.4 could be used for whitewashing houses! It was therefore an act of severe humiliation. Tombs in the ancient world were sacrosanct and their contents were not meant to be disturbed. Some had inscriptions to that effect[4] and we are reminded of the curse of Tutankhamun's tomb in Egypt. Not only did the practice disturb the dead and cut them off from the ancestors; it also obliterated all that remained of them and expunged them from memory and veneration.

We are, of course, unable to identify the *king of Edom*, supposing one such person to be intended.

The punishment of Moab is described in terms similar to but not identical with those applied to Ammon. *Kerioth* was an important if not the capital city, mentioned in the Old Testament only here and in Jer. 48.24. In v. 3 Amos used the word *ruler*, literally 'judge', instead of *king* as in 1.15. This may mean that Moab was not wholly

---

[4] Hayes, *Amos*, pp. 98f.

independent or it may be that the preference for *king* in 1. 15 was due to the desire for word play, as mentioned above.

Against Judah

2.4–5   The crimes of which Judah is accused are very different from those of the other nations so far. They have nothing to do with international relations at all and they are expressed in rather general terms. This in itself is not a sufficiently strong argument against Amos' authorship. As we shall see, Israel's crimes are also committed within Israel. It could be argued that the crimes were different because Judah's responsibility to God was not simply to behave towards other nations in a way which did not breach normal conventions, but, because of the special relationship with God, was also to be obedient to his law and to offer him undivided loyalty. Nor can we regard it as impossible that Amos should be critical of conduct within his own country, for most prophets were. Indeed, if he had been critical of Judah in the course of his preaching in Israel this may have continued to win the approval of his hearers even if it was bringing matters nearer home. We can almost hear the shouts of approval of the earlier oracles against Tyre, Ammon and Moab for instance. They would be echoed, perhaps enthusiastically, after a condemnation of the sister nation of Judah. In spite of all this, however, there are strong grounds for regarding this oracle as coming not from Amos himself but from those later preachers in Judah who recognized that Judah's guilt in this religious sphere was as great as that of the other nations in the political and international spheres.

Phrases like *have spurned the law of the LORD* and *have not observed his decrees* are found predominantly in the writings of the Deuteronomists who were active in the seventh and sixth centuries. Their beliefs were founded upon the book of Deuteronomy and they applied its teachings to the situation in Judah in the last quarter of the seventh century. For many years King Manasseh of Judah had been subject to the Assyrians and had been compelled to conform to their religious practices. When there was discovered in the Temple in 621 BCE a law book which many scholars think to have been at least the legal portion of Deuteronomy (chs. 12–26), Josiah based a series of thoroughgoing

27

reforms on that (II Kings 22 and 23). They appear not to have lasted beyond his death in 609 and so the work of the Deuteronomists continued. Obedience to the law, now a body of legal instructions given by YHWH, and undivided loyalty to YHWH were the keynotes of their teaching, and when during the period of the Babylonian exile they came to write an account of the history of Israel and Judah leading to the fall of Samaria in 722 BCE and of Jerusalem in 587 they assessed each king according to these criteria. A criticism of Judah such as this present one would therefore fit their period and their programme well.

Further, the word translated *false gods* in the same verse, though not common in Deuteronomic writings, is found frequently in Ezekiel. Thus both the language and the content, coupled with the lack of any amplification of the threat of *fire* and of any concluding formula, favour the view that this is not original to Amos.

This does not in any way diminish its value. The fact that the passage can regard disobedience and disloyalty to YHWH to be crimes as serious as those of other nations is a fact of lasting significance and warns against the easy division and categorization of sins.

Against Israel

2.6–16   A similar point emerges from Amos' own attack on Israel, for which the way has now been prepared. Doubtless it would come as a surprise to his hearers. It is, of course, introduced in exactly the same way as the other four (or seven). The crimes of which Israel is accused are, like those of Judah, ones that are committed within Israel by one Israelite against another. They are not described in general terms, however, but as detailed and particular offences. Instead of the usual threat of punishment by fire and the concluding formula there follows here a passage drawing attention to Israel's privileged position (vv. 9–12) which points up even more firmly the enormity of *crime after crime* and makes Israel even more culpable than the surrounding nations. The punishment (vv. 13–18) is therefore all the more severe. Privilege carries with it responsibility and the fact that those whom YHWH delivered from slavery in Egypt and called to be his own were now unwilling to do his will meant that their punishment would be greater. This is a question to which the apostle Paul turns in his letter to the Romans (chs. 9–11) though he sees the possibility of a different outcome.

It is hard to say whether Amos actually intended to list four charges against Israel. By dividing them differently it is possible to discover seven.[5] It depends whether certain pairs of lines are seen as parallel with both lines describing the same *crime* from a slightly different perspective. The question is not all that important, and for convenience, if for no other reason, we shall treat them as four.

The first in v. 6 concerns the treatment of the *honest folk* and *the poor*. No particular class of people is specified as guilty of this mistreatment and we can only speculate as to who is meant by the pronoun *they*. It would help us in this if we could know something of the social structure of Israel in the middle of the eighth century BCE. Archaeological discoveries at Tirzah, which was the capital of Israel for a short time prior to the building of Samaria in the ninth century (I Kings 15.21, 33; 16.8, 15), have shown that some people lived in large houses and some in small ones in the eighth century. Such a division into rich and poor provides a very satisfactory background for Amos' teaching both here and elsewhere. This change in social structure had been coming about gradually ever since Israel had become a nation state under David and it had become acute by the time of Amos. The Israelites who took occupation of the land in the period referred to in the books of Joshua and Judges each had their own piece of land, which was handed down within the family from one generation to the next. With the coming of the monarchy and a more centralized government things began to change. David's capture of further lands and cities from the Canaanites meant that these became royal property. Solomon appointed twelve regional governors who were to supply the court's needs in turn (I Kings 4.4: 7, 27). These needs would be considerable even if the writer of I Kings 4.7ff. was using hyperbole to give an impression of the magnificence of Solomon's court. It seems very likely that the governors and royal landlords began to make demands on their peasant neighbours in order to be able to meet their dues. There may be some supportive evidence for this kind of attitude in the story of the quarrel between Ahab and Naboth in I Kings 21. Ahab wished to

[5] Hayes, *Amos*, p. 107.

possess Naboth's vineyard and was prepared to pay a good price for it, but Naboth was unwilling to let go of his inheritance. Ahab was well aware that there was nothing he could do legally to obtain it and was ready to let the matter rest. Jezebel, however, had Naboth killed so that the vineyard could be incorporated in the royal estate in Jezreel where Ahab had a summer residence. At any rate social anthropologists have shown that in societies like Israel the peasant farmer could fall into debt to his neighbour who lived in the city and earned his living by trade. For whatever reason, then, the peasants fell into a kind of servitude to the wealthy city dwellers. Quite apart from any demands from royal landlords, peasants could get into debt simply because of a poor harvest. There are some examples in the ancient world of interest rates of 40 to 60 per cent per annum. This whole system has been called 'rent capitalism'.[6] The selling of one Israelite to another was permitted under the law in certain circumstances. For instance, Ex. 22.1ff. said that a man found guilty of stealing an ox or sheep which he then killed must repay the cost four times over, and if he was unable to do so he could be sold for his theft. This 'selling' was not exactly slavery, which was forbidden among Israelites, but it did mean that the thief was bound to serve the one he had robbed. What Amos could not tolerate was that *honest folk*, not thieves, were being treated in this way because demands of one kind or another were being made on them, although they were *poor*, by the wealthy landlords and merchants in the towns and cities nearby. The *silver* which may simply mean 'cash' and the *pair of sandals* are either the price paid for the poor by the rich, or the amount of debt into which they had fallen. In Ruth 4.7 and possibly in Ps. 60.8 the casting of a sandal over a piece of land was a symbolic way of ratifying possession of it and similar practices are known to have been common elsewhere in the Ancient Near East. It may carry overtones of that here, though on the whole it seems more likely that *a pair of sandals* indicates a paltry sum. Whether *the poor* and *honest folk* were being sold at a price which devalued them as persons or for a debt which was very small, Amos condemned the practice because it amounted to the exploitation of the poor by the rich and powerful. So it was a *crime*, an act of rebellion against God, in the same category as all the crimes of the other nations.

[6] B. O. Lang, 'The Social Organization of Peasant Poverty in Biblical Israel', *Anthropological Approaches to the Old Testament*, ed. Lang, Fortress Press and SPCK 1985, pp. 83–99.

HONEST

The word translated *honest folk* is an important one for Amos and for the Old Testament in general and it merits a separate note on its meaning. Often it has been translated 'righteous' and Amos has been called 'the prophet of righteousness'. The Hebrew noun is ṣedeq meaning 'righteousness' and the adjective is ṣadîq meaning 'righteous', but often used without a noun to mean 'a righteous person' as here in Amos 2.6. In the first place these words do not in themselves indicate adherence to the law. They are terms used to define a relationship in which people fulfil the obligation placed upon them by the relationship. So a son is 'righteous' when he fulfils his obligations to his father, when he does what a son ought to do. This obligation is not determined by any list of duties which could be hung behind the bedroom door, but by the love and respect that exists between father and son, husband and wife or whatever. Of course, this extends beyond the family to the obligations of God towards the people he has chosen as his own and the obligations of the chosen people towards the God who chose them. So God is 'righteous' when he does what he ought to do for Israel. Sometimes he ought to give them victory over their enemies and there are places where it is legitimate to translate ṣedeq as 'victory' (Isa. 41.2, 10) and especially when it is used in the plural as in Judg. 5.11 where God's 'righteousnesses' are victories given to Israel (REB 'triumphs'). On other occasions, however, because of his people's sin, he ought to punish them and this also is an expression of his ṣedeq.

On the human side persons are ṣadîq when they fulfil their obligations first to God and then to others within the people of God. These obligations rested upon Israel because God had delivered them from Egypt, made them his own, brought them through the desert into Canaan (cf. Amos 2.9–11). Therefore they ought to be grateful, trusting, loyal and obedient to him. The fact that they were now related to each other not only as members of the human race but as members of the people of God meant that they ought to show those same qualities of love, care and generosity as YHWH had shown to them.

Just as it is useful and helpful in a human family if the obligations are spelled out, for example, who does which chore when, so the law was given to Israel to assist the people to fulfil the obligations of being the people of God. But relationships go beyond law and at their best make adherence to rules not an irksome burden but a joyful response to the other person. However, the word *ṣadîq* could be used in a forensic sense to mean 'innocent' in respect of the law, but even here when a person was acquitted with the formula '*ṣadîq* is he' it meant not simply that he had committed no breach of the law but that he remained in a proper and full relationship with his family, tribe or nation.

Finally, the word came to mean 'almsgiving', which is an expression of the obligation of the rich to the poor and not a condescending act of charity.

All this has wide implications for understanding not only Amos or even the rest of the Old Testament but also the New Testament and our own Christian behaviour as well. As those saved by Christ we are under obligation to one another and, since Christ died for all, that obligation extends to all and especially to the deprived. Consequently scripture does not speak of the 'rights' of the poor, or of women, or of slaves, workers or subjects; it speaks consistently of the obligations of the rich, of men, masters and rulers. The 'right' it calls for is to fulfil these obligations.

The second *crime*, in the first half of v. 7, also concerns the underprivileged, *the helpless* and *the humble*. The word translated *helpless* comes from a root which means 'to languish' and refers to people in reduced circumstances. Often it is used as the opposite of 'rich' and should be translated 'poor', but it may have a wider meaning here as REB suggests. It is parallel with the word *humble*, which may also be translated as 'afflicted'. Certainly *humble* does not mean 'those who possess the quality of humility'. Again it has to do with being in *humble* circumstances. In fact the first line of this verse is not easy to translate. The verb translated *grind* sometimes seems to mean 'to pant after' (cf. Jer. 2.24 of 'a she-camel . . . snuffing the wind'). There is a similar verb which means 'to crush' and this is probably intended here. Even so *into the dust* paraphrases rather than translates the Hebrew (literally 'upon dust of earth') and the phrase has probably been added to clarify the meaning of the word translated *grind*. The second line may be rendered more literally 'they turn aside the way of the humble'. This may mean simply that, as REB suggests, they push them out of the way as they walk along the street, or it may mean they obstruct their path to justice, i.e. they make it impossible for the afflicted to take their complaints to the court or to the group of elders who dealt with them in the towns and villages (cf. Ex. 23.6, where the same verb is used). Again, it is not stated who is responsible for this *crime*, but presumably we should think of the powerful in the land who treat the powerless with contempt.

The third *crime*, in the second half of v. 7, is of a different kind. As translated by REB it refers to certain practices in worship which were common enough among the Canaanites and among Israel's present neighbours. There one of the chief concerns of worship was to ensure fertility in the land and this was the result of sexual activity in the divine realm. Worship, therefore, reflected this with priests or other men engaging in sexual intercourse with girls set aside for the purpose. Some think that every girl's first experience of intercourse took place within the context of worship. We know from Hosea (4.10) that such practices also became common in Israel as worship there incorporated Canaanite practices. Hosea calls such girls 'holy women' i.e. women set aside specifically to play their part in worship in this way. The passage in Numbers 25 which recorded how the Israelites first came into contact with the Moabites reflects similar practices at Baal-peor, and Hosea condemns them (Hosea 9.10). The problem with this present verse in Amos is that it doesn't use this same word. It simply speaks of 'the girl' in the singular, and the word used indicates a girl, usually, of marriageable age (cf. for example the use in Deut. 22.23 and frequently). Moreover, although Amos does elsewhere criticize worship at the Israelite shrines (cf. 4.4f.) he never mentions this kind of practice. REB's translation therefore places an interpretation on this line which is scarcely warranted. The Hebrew speaks of one young woman though Amos did call her '*the* young woman'. The half-verse, therefore, is a condemnation of a kind of incest. If a young man was betrothed to a girl then a specific relationship was established into which no one might intrude for sexual purposes (Deut. 22.23, 28–30). If the young man's father had sex with the young woman who thus belonged to his son, that was tantamount to having sex with his daughter-in-law and this was expressly forbidden in Ex. 21.9 and Lev. 18.15. However, what makes this crime so serious was not simply that it is a breach of the law but that it profaned the *holy name* of YHWH; that is, it amounted to a denial of the God whom they worshipped. His *holy name* has become one of these religious clichés whose meaning is rarely questioned. The *name* is sometimes equivalent to YHWH himself, all that he is, and sometimes indicates his reputation among others. In this present instance it makes little difference which meaning we favour. Israelites believed that YHWH was *holy*. This was not just one characteristic among many: it was the very essence of what he was; it was what made him God. Sin of this kind was therefore a denial of the very special nature of God himself and it brought him into disrepute in the eyes of other people. To profane something is to remove it from the sphere of holiness, to rob it of its special quality. In later Judaism the very *name* YHWH came to be regarded as too holy to be found on human lips or heard by human ears. To profane the *holy name*, therefore, is to deny the very nature of YHWH and so destroy his reputation. The crime is as serious as that.

The fourth *crime* (v 8) with its mention of the *altar* and *the house of their God* looks like a wrong connected with worship but a closer look reveals that this is not so. It has been suggested that these two phrases are part of the later reinterpretation of what Amos originally said and so did not form part of his original condemnation.[7] Such a view is hardly necessary. Rather, the crimes, bad in themselves, are being made worse by being associated with religious practice. The two parts of the verse, though different, have enough in common to justify treating them as one crime. *Garments held in pledge* are those which have been handed over to the wealthy money-lender as security for a loan. According to Ex. 22.26f. they should have been handed back to the owner at nightfall, whether or not he had redeemed them, so that he might have something to sleep in. Instead the pawnbrokers were holding on to them and not only so but were lying down in them in the very presence of God *beside every altar*, thus compounding their offence by flouting God and his law. A system of *fines* is not much mentioned in the legal sections of the Old Testament. One reference seems to be in Deut. 22.19, where a man is to be fined a hundred pieces of silver for giving a bad name to a woman by falsely accusing her of not being a virgin when he married her. The other is in Ex. 21.22 where a man who knocks down a pregnant woman in a brawl and causes a miscarriage must pay 'whatever fine the woman's husband demands'. From these two instances it would seem that fines were paid to the injured party as compensation. Here we should probably think of either the judiciary or the priests who awarded and collected the fines as holding on to

[7] H. W. Wolff, *Amos*, p. 166.

them and spending them on wine which they then drank in the *house of God* itself. Both these things are therefore breaches of the law but the wrong consists not merely in that but in a rejection of YHWH's authority and even in flagrant defiance of him.

Although all these crimes of Israel may reflect parts of the law which were being broken in Israel, the chief complaint of Amos was that they showed a totally wrong attitude to YHWH. Instead of showing gratitude by obedience and right living they had proved themselves to be no better than their neighbours, whom they were quick enough to condemn. If the latter had not lived and behaved according to their lights, neither had Israel lived according to the clearer light afforded by its relationship with YHWH.

This point was then reinforced by a reminder of all that YHWH had done for them, which only serves to rub in the seriousness of their offence. The passage in vv. 9–12 shows some curious features. In the first place the events described are not in chronological order. Verse 9 deals with the occupation of Canaan. Verse 10 goes further back to the exodus from Egypt followed by a reference to the time in *the wilderness*. Then another reference to the settlement (v. 10) carries the story of Israel further forward with a reference in v. 11 to *prophets* and *Nazirites*. Verse 12 picks up the theme of disregard for and even the restraint of both these groups of messengers of YHWH. Further, in v. 9 Israel is referred to in the third person, while in vv. 10–12 the nation is addressed directly in the second person. This has led some to the conclusion that Amos himself spoke only v. 9, and that vv. 10–12 are a part of the later preaching and interpretative process. There is some support for this also in the fact that the *forty years . . . in the wilderness* are not mentioned anywhere else in the prophetic writings. If these verses are an extension of what Amos actually said they serve only to underline his intention, which was to remind Israel of God's goodness on their behalf. The *fruit above* and the *root below* are simply equivalent to our 'root and branch'. *Amorites* is just another name for the Canaanites who inhabited the land before Israel. In the genealogical list in Gen. 10 Canaan is the father of the Amorites (v. 16). Precisely who are meant by the *prophets* is not clear. If Amos said this it must refer to his predecessors such as Elijah whom Ahab sought to silence along with others unnamed (I Kings 18.7–17). If the verses originated later it could include people like Amos himself (7.10–14) and Jeremiah (cf. 33.1). The form of the prohibition here is a very strong one like that of the Ten Commandments ('You shall

not . . .') and that which Amaziah sought to impose on Amos
(7.12–14). The *Nazirites* are less frequently mentioned. Their name is
derived from a verb meaning 'to dedicate' or 'consecrate' and Num. 6
sets out regulations relating to them. As part of their vow they were
to avoid drinking wine, touching corpses and cutting the hair.
Samson is described as one, not because he himself made a vow but
because of his mother's abstinence before his birth. He was to 'strike
the first blow for Israel's freedom' (Judg. 13.2–5; cf. 16.17). The terms
of the vow tended and perhaps were intended to preserve their
separation from all things Canaanite. Amos' charge was that YHWH's
gift of *prophets* and *Nazirites* to guide Israel and keep them on track
had been spurned.

The actual threat against Israel follows in vv. 13–16. It opens with
a verse containing a word which occurs nowhere else in the Old
Testament and which REB translates as *groan* in the first line and *creak*
in the second line of v. 13. This means that v. 13 describes YHWH's
feelings and the actual punishment begins in v. 14. Others translate
as 'press down' in which case the punishment begins at v. 13 with
the threat that YHWH will press down on Israel just as a heavy cart
presses down on the ground beneath its wheels. It is not easy to
decide which is correct. In any case the punishment in vv. 14–16 is
described differently in terms of utter and complete defeat in battle.
Troops will have nowhere to run and, even if they do run away, not
one will be saved. Although Amos used military language it is not
certain that he was expecting such an attack on Israel. He may have
been speaking metaphorically. Even if it is understood literally there
is no indication in the text as to who will mount the attack. Probably
when he spoke there was no nation in a position to do so. Amos'
certainty of divine judgment was based nor upon observation of the
current international situation, nor on the availability of a nation to
be God's instrument of judgment, but upon the belief that God was
righteous – did what was right – and this meant that he must punish
and reject his chosen people when they did things which broke those
relationships which ought to exist within his people.

Israel's sins and threatened punishment

Amos 3.1–4.13

Introduction

3.1 This verse marks the beginning of a new section of the book. The same call to *listen* occurs at the very beginning of chs. 4 and 5. It seems that those who compiled the book intended their readers to take these sayings of Amos together, whether or not the prophet actually spoke them all on the same occasion. Even if we look at each section in the chapter separately we ought also to see them in relation to each other. REB has tidied up this first verse slightly by rendering the last phrase *which he brought up from Egypt*, whereas the Hebrew has the first person 'I' in this part of the verse alongside the third person, LORD, in the earlier part. Perhaps the Judaean editors wished to make it clear that the *Israelites* to whom Amos had spoken must now be seen to include *the whole nation*, i.e. Israel *and* Judah, and they used the first person 'I' because that was the conventional way of referring to the exodus.

Privilege and punishment

3.2–11 This section begins with a startling verse in which God, through his prophet, affirms his relationship with his people but, instead of making this the foundation of his care and protection, he now gives it as the basis for his punishment. It begins by asserting the specially privileged position of Israel. The word behind *cared for* is often translated as 'known'. It is part of election vocabulary and so here denotes the special relationship between YHWH and his chosen people (see note on Hosea 4.1–3). As we saw in the comments on 2.6–16, this carried with it responsibilities which Israel all too readily forgot. Their belief that God had brought them out of Egypt and given them possession of the land of Canaan led them to expect his unconditional help and protection. Instead they were now told by Amos that YHWH's care for them in this way made them all the more culpable when they failed to live as the people of God. *That is why*, or 'therefore', is the common way of introducing a threat for which Amos' hearers would be totally unprepared.

3.3–8 There now follows a series of rhetorical questions all expecting the answer 'No' and based on a method of teaching which was common in Wisdom circles (cf. Job 38). Since the LORD is referred to in the third person we must see these verses as coming from the prophet's own mind and not as part of the divine message. Their relation to v. 2 is not altogether clear and much depends on where we see the climax of the series. First, by leaving a space after v. 6 REB may be suggesting the climax falls there. Verses 3–6 are then examples of pairs of things which belong together as cause and effect. These are now used to support the statement in v. 2 that God's punishment had its cause in the fact that he cared for Israel. So the final example is of disaster befalling a city and caused by YHWH. On any reckoning v. 7, which is in prose, rather interrupts the series of questions. This interpretation, however, leaves v. 8 also hanging in the air. Second, we may see v. 8 as the climax to the series with v. 7 an interruption to which we must return later. Then the whole series of rhetorical questions is meant to illustrate and lead up to the fact that when YHWH speaks to his prophet his prophet must pass on the message. But in this case we are left without any clear connection between v. 2 and vv. 3–8. By using a little imagination it is possible to bridge this gap. Amos' proclamation of God's word in v. 2 would be most likely to evoke a hostile response from his audience: 'Who does he think he is to make such a statement?' In this way perhaps they questioned his competence and his authority as a prophet. We know from passages like I Kings 22 that there were some prophets who were always willing to offer a pleasing prophecy to the king (see also Jer. 27 and 28) but that sometimes there was one who had the courage to say what YHWH had told him even if it meant contradicting the majority and predicting disaster. Amos was in such a position and it would be natural for his authority to be questioned. His response, however, is to show how it was accepted that in the natural world one event inevitably causes another and to claim a similar inevitability with regard to his prophesying: *The Lord God has spoken; who will not prophesy?* The question of authority will arise again in a very personal way in ch. 7.12–14. On the whole this second view seems to be the better way of understanding the passage.

Now we must return to v. 7. There are three considerations which should make us doubt whether it is part of Amos' original speech. First it cannot easily be rendered as poetry and REB rightly prints it as prose; second, it is in the form of a statement and not a question; and third, it robs v. 8 of its effect if we are right in thinking that vv. 3–8 are a response to a questioning of his authority. It is better, therefore, to regard it as a later comment but that is no reason for disregarding what it says. It, too, speaks of the relationship between YHWH and his prophet. There is evidence from the books of Deuteronomy and Jeremiah that the question was exercising the minds of people in Judah in the seventh century BCE. The threat to Jerusalem made it essential to be able to distinguish between a true prophet and a false one. Deuteronomy 18.15–22 raises the issue but the conclusion in v. 22 is not terribly helpful. 'When a word spoken by a prophet in the name of the LORD is not fulfilled and does not come true, it is not a word spoken by the LORD.' In Jer. 27 and 28, where Jeremiah and Hananiah give conflicting messages from YHWH, even Jeremiah himself is forced to retire for further thought before he can be sure that it is his message which really is God's word. Here the author of this verse claims that the true prophet is the confidant of God. The word rendered *plan* is a word most commonly found in Wisdom circles. It denotes first a circle of intimate friends and then the counsel or advice that they give. So the prophet is let into the secret of God's plans which are revealed to him but remain hidden from others outside the circle. Whatever God decides to do he tells his prophet so that he in turn may warn others. Prophets are therefore 'in the know' and when God's plans come to fruition they will be seen to have been 'in the know'.

Since Amos had threatened punishment in v. 2 and had asserted his authority as a prophet in vv. 3–8 we should expect him now to make clear what the punishment would be. Before he did so, however, he made some observations of his own in vv. 9–10. In spite of the concluding formula at the end of v. 10 these are not introduced as a word from YHWH. Moreover in the Hebrew the concluding formula does not appear at the end of v. 10 but in the middle of it! It is probably best to omit it altogether rather than simply change its place. Then Amos called upon his audience to travel in imagination to *Ashdod*, one of the Philistine cities, and *Egypt*, to stand on the *palaces* or fortifications there and to proclaim an invitation for their people to come and see what was going on in Samaria. The implication is that even these people, and we don't know why *Ashdod and Egypt* were chosen, would recognize as evil the terrible things that were happening there. There is *tumult*, (the very opposite of *shalom*) and *oppression*. There is *violence* against persons and *plundering* of property, the gains from which they store up for themselves. It may well be that the envoys from the two nations are intended to be the witnesses necessary to prove the guilt of the accused (cf. Deut. 19.15).

3.11 Now, at last, the judgment of YHWH could be given. The *land* would be surrounded, the *stronghold* broken down and the loot they had hoarded in their palaces as a result of their plundering would be carried off. As usual in Amos the punishment is quite vividly expressed but remains imprecise. There is no indication as to who the *enemy* is.

3.12 This is a very difficult verse to translate and to interpret. As REB translates, it is promised that the *Israelites in Samaria* would *be rescued*. This is not impossible, for v. 11 had spoken only of the encirclement of the land, the demolition of the stronghold and the carrying off of loot. It had not threatened the decimation or the exile of the people. In the context of the whole book, however, it is difficult to think of Amos promising deliverance to the wealthy in Samaria, especially in view of 4.1–8. It is better to begin by seeing whether the verse may be construed as a further threat. The first two lines are clear enough once they are seen against the background of Ex 22.10–13. A shepherd was responsible for the sheep in his charge. If he lost a sheep and there were no witnesses then he might have to pay the owner since he might in fact have stolen it. If it had been attacked and killed by a wild beast then he did not have to pay, but in order to prove that this was what had happened he had to return the carcase to the owner as evidence. As a sheep breeder Amos would have been well aware of this. He had also seen the attack on Israel in terms of a lion roaring (1.2; 3.8) the lion being YHWH himself. So the first half of the verse simply draws the picture of a shepherd obtaining the necessary evidence that the sheep has been attacked and eaten by a wild animal. The questions begin to arise in the second half of the verse, where REB footnote admits that the

Hebrew is obscure, especially in the last line. The third line of the Hebrew simply claims that *Israelites will be rescued*, and we should probably understand this to mean that a few Israelites would survive as evidence that the rest had been destroyed or carried off. The word 'rescue' in this line may even have a touch of irony about it. The last line then describes these few as living or sitting in Samaria on something or other. What they were sitting on is almost impossible to say. REB is one possible attempt and there have been many others, some of which do not suggest the luxury implied in the present text. An alternative translation may therefore be:

> As a shepherd rescues from a lion's mouth
> Two knuckle bones or the tip of an ear
> So some Israelites will be 'rescued',
> Who sit in Samaria
> On the edge of a bed or on a silken cushion.

It has to be emphasized that any translation of the second half of the verse must be tentative but the likelihood is that the weight of the verse should fall on destruction and not on deliverance.

3.13–15   These verses offer a further threat of punishment. Imaginary people, or more probably the envoys from *Ashdod* and *Egypt* of v. 9, were now called as witnesses to *testify* as in a court of law against the Israelites. Such testimony to what they had seen could result in one verdict only, that of guilty, and so there followed the sentence of punishment. The first part of this in v. 14 was directed against the royal shrine at *Bethel*. Although the capital was Samaria and there was probably a shrine there, Bethel remained the most important religious centre and the main festivals in which the king took part were held there. In 7.13 it is called *the king's sanctuary, a royal shrine*. The word of YHWH through Amos was that he would *deal with Israel* and *with the altars of Bethel*. The word translated *deal with* more literally means 'to visit', and YHWH may be expected to visit his shrine for the good of his people. But he may also visit to bring disaster, and when the verb is followed by the preposition used in this verse ('visit upon . . .') it is equivalent to 'punish'. *The horns of the altar* were perhaps the most sacred part. The term refers to the projections at each corner of the altar to which people guilty of unintentionally causing the death of another, i.e. of manslaughter, could cling for protection from those bent on revenge (cf. Ex. 21.12ff.), where the appointed place is clearly part of the altar). After the coronation of Solomon David's general Joab, who had supported Adonijah's claim to the throne took 'hold of the horns of the altar' for sanctuary against any purge. Benaiah, on the instructions of Solomon, still killed him there on the ground that he had killed two other 'innocent men . . . without . . . David's knowledge' (I Kings 2.28ff.). Now at Bethel there would be no place of safety for Israel, for the *horns of the altar* would *be hacked off*. Verse 15 deals with the residences of the royal court, which was in Samaria even though the city is not mentioned here. It therefore follows on from the earlier oracles against the capital. The *winter houses* and the *summer residences* may be a reference to two-storey buildings, one storey for each season of the year according to climate, but more probably they refer to a winter palace in Samaria itself and to a summer residence in the country, for example, in Jezreel, where Ahab appears to have had one (I Kings 21. 1, 8; cf. II Kings 8.29; 9.15). The presence of *houses adorned with ivory* in Samaria a century earlier in the time of Ahab is attested by I Kings 22.39 and by the discovery by archaeologists in 1910 and again just after the First World War of a vast quantity of ivory ornaments and decorations (see Introduction, p.6). The *great houses* is an inclusive summary term, unless the common word *great* has accidentally been substituted for the similar but rare word 'ebony' (cf. Ezek. 27.15) which would make an excellent parallel with *ivory*.

Although Amos, in common with most if not all the pre-exilic prophets, never explicitly differentiated between guilty and inno-cent, oppressor and oppressed, when he described the judgment of God, but rather saw the disaster as befalling the whole nation (God deals *with Israel*) it was to the former that he addressed his criticism and his threats. Notice again that it is 'I', i.e. YHWH, who will bring judgment and that no human agent at all is mentioned.

Chapter 4 may be divided into four separate sayings. First, there is a threat against the wealthy women of Samaria (vv. 1–3), followed by a criticism of the worship currently offered at Bethel and Gilgal (vv. 4–5). Next comes a list of disasters which should have acted as a warning to Israel but which failed to bring about the required change of behaviour (vv. 6–11). Finally there is a terrible threat (vv. 12–13). There is probably some connection between these four sections although it is not always as clear as we might wish. Whether they were all spoken by Amos on the same occasion or whether a later editor arranged Amos' sayings in this manner we cannot be sure, except that there is some evidence of editorial activity.

Against the wealthy women

4.1–3   This, then, concerned the wealthy women of Samaria. He calls them *Bashan cows*. The word *cows* is used of women nowhere else in the Old Testament and we must beware of reading into it all the pejorative sense it has now come to have in colloquial English. It is hardly a flattering metaphor, but the main emphasis is on the excesses of the women. *Bashan* was a fertile area to the east of the Jordan and was famous for its good quality cattle (cf. Ps. 22.12). Like the well-fed and fat cows which Bashan produced, the wealthy women associated with the court in Samaria had grown rich and lived in indolent luxury at the expense of the *poor* and *helpless* (cf. 2.6–7). Their oppression would not be direct, for they themselves were not likely to have been in positions of leadership or power. Indeed Amos drew a picture of them sitting at home or at their parties calling on their menfolk, their *lords*, to *bring* them *drink* bought with the spoils of injustice, and demanding more and more, their greed never satisfied. Through their demands they encourage their *lords* to *oppress the helpless* yet more. REB has carefully and properly avoided the word 'husbands' found in some translations (e.g. RSV). The word never means 'husband' (though REB uses 'husband' at Gen. 18.12). The women here are almost certainly not only the wives of courtiers, but concubines and courtesans as well. He thus presents a picture of an extravagant and decadent court which not only ignores but exacerbates the poverty of the poor.

YHWH's threat against the women is introduced by a strong formula. Instead of *this is the word of the LORD* he uses the form of an oath *the Lord GOD has sworn by his holiness*. An oath does not necessarily belong in a legal context; it is the most solemn form of promise and is usually validated by reference to a person in a superior position. A servant may swear by his lord or a subject by his king. YHWH's promise or threat is similarly validated but since there is no one superior to him on whom he can call he calls upon *his holiness*. As we have seen (cf. 2.7) this refers to his own divine nature, all that he is in himself as God. A little later on, in 6.8, he does in fact, swear *by himself*. No threat could therefore be more solemn than this. It is as though YHWH is laying his very being on the line if he should fail to carry out his judgment on the women in Samaria. The threat is that they and their children will be carried out of the city through the *breaches* made *in the wall* by an enemy and thrown on the *dunghill*, probably already dead. Again there is no indication as to the identity of those who would break through the walls. Nor can we say how the women were carried away. The translation *shields* is supported by I Sam. 17.7, where the same word is found, but in Prov. 22.5 (REB 'snares'), Num. 33.5 and Josh. 23.13 it seems to refer to something sharp like a barb or thorn. Also the word translated *fish-baskets* may mean a large pot (II Kings 4.38), but it may also mean a thorn (Isa. 34.13; Hosea 2.6). However, whether they were to be carried away in some sort of container or on some sort of spike it made little difference! The end is the same. As the footnote in REB points out, the Hebrew actually says they will be *thrown* out on *the Harmon*. What this meant we do not know. It could possibly refer to Mount Hermon but that seems a curious place for them to be thrown. A division of the consonants would provide 'hill of Rimmon' and we can read in Judg. 20.45, 47; 21.13, of the Rock of Rimmon which was where the six hundred survivors fled after the massacre of the Benjaminites. If it is not a known place REB may be correct to translate *dunghill*. Again, it does not make a lot of difference to the sense. Hayes is probably right to suggest that it is not exile that is threatened but the transporting from the city of the dead bodies of the women killed in the battle for the city. Instead of a decent and proper burial the bodies would be thrown out on the *dunghill* or whatever.[1] At all events this ignominious end would be brought about by YHWH.

Worship at Bethel and Gilgal

4.4–5 From the capital Amos next switched his attention to the shrines at *Bethel* and *Gilgal*. As we have seen, the former was the royal shrine where the corrupt court of vv. 1–3 would go, especially

---

[1] Hayes, *Amos*, p. 140.

on festival occasions, to worship God. It was one of two shrines
established by Jeroboam I in 922 BCE when Israel seceded from Judah.
The other was at Dan but, probably because of its geographical
location in the far north, it played a secondary role to Bethel, which
had a long history going back in tradition to Jacob himself (Gen. 28).
It was therefore a very natural choice. In both centres Jeroboam I
erected golden bulls. As far as the historian of Kings was concerned
this made Jeroboam I into a reprobate figure with whom all later
kings of Israel were compared. The two national shrines had come
to be regarded as schismatic, and the bulls as idolatrous representations of Baal. It is virtually certain that this was never Jeroboam's
intention. Prior to his becoming king in Israel, he is presented as a
true and ardent Yahwist, opposed to Solomon's policy of using free
Israelites as a kind of slave labour in the building of the Temple and
palace. Moreover Kings still records (I Kings 11) how he was chosen
by YHWH through a prophet Ahijah to be king over the Northern
tribes. Once a separate kingdom had been established it was vital to
provide a national shrine to replace Jerusalem, which was now in
Judah, and what better place than Bethel for the central tribes and
Dan for those in the north, the so-called Galilean tribes. Further,
since the Ark was in the Jerusalem Temple a substitute had to be
found. The Ark was seen as the throne of YHWH and the bulls at
Bethel and Dan were doubtless meant to fulfil the same function.
These were not originally seen as representations of anyone; they
were simply thrones for the invisible YHWH. Perhaps with hindsight
the bull was an unwise choice, for it did have associations with Baal.
Whether Judaean Amos regarded the shrine at *Bethel* as schismatic
we shall have to consider later, but it is worth saying here and now
that he never mentioned the bull in his criticism of worship at Bethel.
Some years later Hosea did (Hos. 8.5; 10.5). *Gilgal* also had a long
history. In tradition it was the first stopping place on the west bank
of the Jordan when Joshua and his followers entered Canaan (Josh.
4.19) and the first Passover in the Promised Land was celebrated
there (Josh. 5). So far as Israel was concerned therefore, both shrines
had better credentials than Jerusalem, which had fallen into Israelite
hands only in the time of David (II Sam. 5) and had been a Jebusite
city up to that time. This would make Amos' attack on the worship
there all the harder to bear, though attack it he did.

He began (v. 4) with an invitation to worship there which probably
echoed the priestly invitation (cf. Ps. 100.2 where 'enter his presence'

is literally 'come before him'). We are not told what the occasion was. It may have been the Feast of Tabernacles or one of the other festivals. The shocking thing is that no sooner does he announce the invitation than he denounces the worship there as an infringement of YHWH's law. It is a pity in some ways that REB has chosen this translation which, be it said, is not incorrect, but which does obscure the connection with what has gone before. It would perhaps have been better to have rendered it 'commit a crime', for it is the verb from which the noun is derived in chs. 1 and 2. Not only the social injustices but the worship at the royal sanctuary was a 'crime', an act of rebellion against God. The same is true of that at Gilgal. What was it that made it a 'crime'? The second half of v. 4 and v. 5 make it clear that there was nothing wrong with the performance. They were offering the *sacrifices for the morning* (cf. I Sam 1.19); they were fulfilling Jacob's vow at Bethel to give *tithes* to YHWH (Gen. 28.22); they were offering cakes *without leaven* as a *thankoffering* (Lev. 6.16; 7.12) and *freewill-offerings* (i.e. spontaneous offerings – cf. Ex. 35.29). They were certainly fulfilling all their religious duties there, and it is even possible to interpret these verses in such a way that they were exceeding their duties. Why, then, was it a 'crime'? Various suggestions have been made. It may have been because Amos believed the proper place for all these things was in the Temple in Jerusalem. In other words he regarded the Israelite shrines as schismatic, as later Judeans certainly did,[2] but Amos gave no indication of that, nor did he make any suggestion that they should offer their worship at Zion. Or it may have been because the worship at the sanctuary was at odds with their lives in society, where they practised all kinds of injustice. If we see a strong connection between vv. 1–3 and 4–6 we might say that it is the *lords* of the *Bashan cows* who are invited to *Bethel* to commit a crime. Certainly later on, in 5.21, Amos condemned worship which was not accompanied by proper ethical behaviour in everyday life. In actual fact the reason given in the text in v. 6 is simply that Israelites *love to do* it. That does not in itself preclude the reasons just given but it certainly does not make them explicit, and if we take the words as we have them we may say that Amos condemned the worship at *Bethel* and *Gilgal* because people who came loved the worship. Just as they enjoyed the luxury of life at court, so they enjoyed the practices of worship, the processions, the

---

[2] Polley, *Amos*, pp. 101, 109ff.

sacrifices, the crowds. We should then understand him to be saying that worship is not a matter of performing correct actions or even exaggeratedly elaborate ones; it is a glad, free and grateful response to God. When the 'liturgy', whatever form it takes, replaces God as the object of love, then worship becomes a 'crime'. It is very unlikely that Amos was advocating a religion without any set forms of worship, but the forms should have been the vehicle by which the people expressed their love and gratitude to God and not ends in themselves.

Unheeded Warnings

4.6–11 Instead of the expected threat we find a poem of five stanzas, each one ending with the same refrain. For the moment the threat was delayed while Amos reminded the people of opportunities for repentance which had been given to them. These had taken the form of natural disasters. The first, v. 6, was *starvation* and *famine*. The Hebrew actually has a very vivid expression 'cleanness of teeth'. This was no mere accidental phenomenon. The 'I', as REB suggests, is emphatic. Like the remaining four this had been sent by YHWH as a warning but it had no effect -*Yet you did not come back to me.* The second, v. 7, was drought. If we were being pedantic we could say that this should have come first as the cause of the *famine*, but Amos was not concerned with such niceties. Since *harvest* was in the spring, the rains which failed *three months* earlier were the heavy winter rains which provided the basic growing conditions. It was not total drought, however. The rain was patchy. Some regions had it, others did not. Those which did not were short of drinking water and staggered to other towns where there was enough to drink. This warning too was ineffective. The third, v. 9, was crop disease followed by pests affecting particularly the summer fruit harvest. The precise nature of the *blight* is uncertain but is not important. Again, it seems to be associated with the lack of rain and the hot scorching wind. This was accompanied by swarms of *locusts*, to which Amos returned in the account of his first vision (7.1) and which can be seen to have occurred not infrequently. The effect was quite devastating, leaving a whole area stripped bare in a very short time. They featured among the plagues in Egypt (Ex. 10.1–20), and Joel 1 and 2.1–11 make clear their prevalence. The fourth (v. 10) is, in fact, a *plague* described as *like the plagues of Egypt*. It may be that the reference to locusts brought to Amos' mind *the plagues of Egypt* unless, as some think, this phrase was added by the editor to emphasize the seriousness of the warning. Rhythmically it does overload the line somewhat. Curiously the text switches from *plague* apparently to warfare and the reference to *the sword*. It may be, however, that this is used metaphorically to speak of the people being struck down with plague. Certainly the fact that the *camps* stank seems to suggest plague. It is worth remembering, too, that in Joel 1 and 2 the locusts are described as an invading army. *Your troops of horses* is also a battle figure. There is, however, another possibility. Another Hebrew word with exactly the same consonants as *sword* means 'desolation'. Further, *with the sword(?) I slew your young men* makes a complete line of poetry but leaves *your troops of horses* as a phrase hanging in the air. It is quite likely that when the Hebrew word *ḥereb* was understood as *sword* instead of desolation the readers added the phrase about the *horses*. Either of these explanations is better than Hayes' belief that some defeat in battle is intended.[3] He does point out, however, that plagues serious enough to have found their way into Assyrian records occurred in Assyria in 765 and 759 BCE near enough to the time of Amos and these may have affected Israel. The final warning was of *destruction*. The comparison with *Sodom and Gomorrah* not only emphasizes its severity but also suggests a similar catastrophe. The word translated *destruction* really refers to a 'turning over' and therefore many think this is a description of an earthquake. We should remember, though, that the earthquake of 1.1 was still two years in the future. In any case both here and in Gen. 19.23ff. the main emphasis is on fire. Great as the disaster was, Israel was *like a brand snatched from the burning*. Even that was insufficient to bring them to their senses and to God.

We are entitled to ask just when these five events occurred. It could be that they were all stages in one calamity, drought which led to *famine,blight* and *locusts, plague* and destruction by *fire*. We have to say that we do not know of any such series of events. Famine and drought were by no means unknown and a very severe occurrence took place a century earlier in the time of Elijah (I Kings 18). Locusts and blight were probably not uncommon. In the curious passage in

[3] Hayes, *Amos*, p. 147.

6.9–10 Amos seems to refer to a threat of plague, while *fire* was the judgment befalling the foreign nations in chs. 1 and 2. It is not impossible, therefore, that Amos knew of some such incidents in the recent past. Others have pointed out that the passage bears some resemblance to certain 'curse' passages, for instance in Lev. 26.14ff. and Deut. 28.15ff., and suggest that Amos may have been using this curse tradition to describe the warnings YHWH had given to Israel. The passages in Leviticus and Deuteronomy certainly speak of similar disasters but the similarities are hardly sufficient to suggest dependence. In any case Amos was speaking about the past and not the future and his words would not have carried much weight unless his audience had been able to recognize specific events to which he was referring. The fact that we cannot identify them should not surprise us, for our information about what happened in Israel is scanty.

To recap briefly: Amos has described the sins of the women in Samaria and threatened them with death and ignominy; he has criticized the worship at Bethel and Gilgal; he has reminded the people that they have already had several warnings which they had failed to recognize and therefore to heed. Now the moment had arrived to pronounce judgment.

A terrible threat

4.12–13 This judgment is introduced by the customary *therefore*. The expectation of its severity is heightened by the repetition of *this is what I shall do* and what follows looks like a weak anticlimax – *Prepare to meet your God*. At least we should have expected a terrible threat of destruction even if we had learned by now not to expect a precise identification of the agent of destruction.

H. W. Wolff[4] has suggested the *this* was spoken with the finger pointing at the destroyed city of Bethel as a threat of what would happen to Jerusalem. This means, of course, that the verse could not have come from Amos but has been added by later preachers or editors when Jerusalem was in danger in the latter part of the seventh

---

[4] Wolff, *Amos*, p. 222.

century. Such a radical view is not necessary. It is quite possible to see the verse as the culmination of Amos' speech in a threat to Bethel itself. The *this* refers not to Bethel (or Samaria or any other city) but to what follows, to '*Prepare to meet your God.*' YHWH will bring about an encounter with himself. The word 'prepare' is very often used of preparing for battle (e.g. Ezek. 38.7) and the sentence would therefore conjure up the thought of a confrontation between YHWH and Israel. Traditionally YHWH has been on Israel's side waging war against its enemies. To be called to *prepare to meet* him in battle would therefore be astonishing (cf. Isa. 28.21) and disastrous. The word is also used of preparing for worship (e.g. II Chron. 35.4). In proper circumstances nothing could be better than to *meet* God in worship, but with a record like theirs this, too, would be disastrous.

So, having ignored all YHWH's warnings, having refused to come back to him, they are now confronted with the prospect of coming to meet him in their self-gratification. Having *come* to Bethel and Gilgal with the intention of enjoying themselves rather than of meeting with God they must now *meet* him, as those who have rebelled. Far from being an anticlimax, therefore, this verse carries a very serious and dreadful threat. The seriousness of meeting God in this frame of mind finds expression also in the New Testament (cf. passages like Matt. 25.31–46; Rom. 2.2–6; Heb. 10.26–31).

The subsequent v. 13 is one of three hymn-like passages found in the book of Amos. The others are at 5.8f. and 9.6. It is often questioned whether these verses do really come from Amos or were included by later editors. In favour of the latter view it is pointed out that the word translated *creates* is found elsewhere only in texts which are generally thought to come from the sixth century (e.g. Gen. 1.1; Isa. 40.26). However it may well be that those sixth-century writers were using language which belonged essentially in the context of worship and had hitherto been little used outside it. Since this is a hymn-like passage it would be natural to use it here. Or it may be argued that to add anything to v. 12 as interpreted above would be to weaken its impact, but whoever placed it here, Amos or the editor, did not think so. In fact, what the verse does is to reinforce the idea of the majesty and power of the God Israel must *prepare to meet*, and so heighten the sense of awe at such a meeting. The third line of the verse – *and declares his thoughts to mankind* – though a possible meaning, does not fit the context well, and the meaning of the word translated *thoughts* is uncertain. An alternative reading of the Hebrew by redividing the consonants would produce 'who causes vegetation to grow in the ground'(cf Gen. 2.5). In the fourth line REB has also added the words *with thick clouds* which do not appear in the Hebrew. It is better to read, along with the early Greek translation, the Septuagint, 'He who made dawn <u>and</u> darkness'. The God whom Israel must *prepare to meet* is the great creator of the world, even *YHWH the God of Hosts*. The *Hosts* have sometimes been thought to be the heavenly hosts of stars and planets, and since the phrase *God of Hosts* occurs here in a passage dealing with creation, it could be argued that this is the meaning Amos had in mind. However, the word *Hosts* has to do primarily with 'armies' and the phrase sees YHWH as God of the armies. Whether this refers to Israel's armies or to the superhuman beings who serve YHWH as their king we cannot be sure. In either case the armies are usually there to fight for or to protect Israel. Here, however, Israel must meet this God of the armies as its enemy.

Israel and Yahweh

Amos 5.1 – 6.14

Like the previous two chapters this also begins with a call to *listen* which suggests the opening of a new section. Where the section ends is more difficult to decide, but v. 17 seems an appropriate place. There are several smaller sections within this which may show some pattern. Again it is not possible to say whether Amos spoke them all on one occasion or whether the arrangement is due to the editor.

A Lament

5.1–3

5.1–2 The opening poem is described as a *dirge* or lament. Such poems have their own form. They consist of pairs of lines usually with three beats in the first and two in the second, though this cannot always be maintained in translation. To give an impression we might translate the first two lines as;

> Fallen no more to rise
> Virgin Israel

Needless to say the metre is used to a considerable extent in the book of Lamentations (cf. also I Sam. 1.19–27).

The *dirge* was sung or spoken as the prophet's own word and not as a word from YHWH. So sure is he of Israel's approaching end that he can lament the death as though it had happened. That end will come while Israel, personified as a female, is still metaphorically a *virgin*. The word is not used to denote Israel's purity, for she is anything but pure. Rather the emphasis is on her comparative youth and immaturity. It will happen before she is grown up. (For an extended use of this metaphor cf. Ezek. 16.) Strictly speaking the Hebrew means *'virgin of Israel'* and since cities are often personified in the feminine the phrase may refer to the city of Samaria rather than to Israel the nation. This makes better sense of the phrase that she is *prostrate* in her own land; the fact that there is *no one to lift her up* may simply mean that she is beyond human help or it may imply that YHWH himself, who is traditionally Israel's protector, will absent himself at this critical moment, when the capital most needs him (cf. 3.2).

5.3 The prophet could sing his dirge because of *the words of the Lord* GOD which he had heard. *Thousand, hundred* and *ten* are all military units, say 'division', 'company' and 'detachment'. As translated by REB the oracle means that the military strength of the city would be reduced almost to nothing. The emphasis is not on the the the 'detachment' left but on the 'division' which would be defeated. The problem with this translation is that the verb translated *will have . . . left* is active and not passive and since the verb is feminine *the city*, a feminine noun, must be the subject. So *the city . . .* will leave a company or detachment for the 'house of Israel'. This may mean the city will make them available for national use or for use by the 'dynasty' (house) of Israel; so the verse remains a threat to the military resources of Israel.

Attendance at shrines and seeking Yahweh

5.4–6   Next there follows, as another divine word, a further strong condemnation of Israel's worship at *Bethel* and *Gilgal* (cf. 4.14). The present text also mentions *Beersheba*, a sanctuary in the far south of Judah. Whether Israelites from the North visited this shrine must remain in some doubt. It is certainly not mentioned in the threat in the second half of the verse and although REB has managed to compress it into the second line of the verse it really constitutes a third (extra) line. It may be better therefore to regard it as having been added to the other two by some later Judaean preacher who was using Amos' words and applying them also to *Beersheba*. The word translated *make your way to* is often rendered 'seek' and is used for going to worship. Indeed the REB loses something of the terseness of this passage which is retained by versions like RSV.

> Seek me and live
> Do not seek Bethel
> Do not come to Gilgal
> Do not cross over to Beersheba.

There are two possible interpretations of these prohibitions. First, as a Judaean Amos may have considered Jerusalem as the place where YHWH was to be 'sought', for this was where he might be found (cf. Pss. 46–48). Then the verses would be a condemnation of these shrines as schismatic. We recognized this as a possibility with 4.4ff. Second, as we argued in the case of 4.4ff., it is more likely that Amos was condemning attendance at the shrines because this had become a substitute for 'seeking' YHWH himself. Mere performance of rites would not bring life. Only the frequent and regular meeting with God through the rites would do so.

LIFE

Life in the Old Testament, of course, has to do with being alive in a physical sense as in the story of the raising to life of the widow's son by Elijah at Zarephath (I Kings 17.17ff.), but in many contexts it is not simply a matter of a beating heart or a breathing lung. Life, and its opposite, death, have a wider meaning than that. We ourselves frequently use the words to express quality of life rather than its mere presence or absence, and this is true of the Old Testament as well. This is particularly true of the 'Wisdom' books such as Proverbs, Ecclesiastes and Job, but it is true also of all other parts of the Old Testament. One way of thinking about this, though like most analogies it does not work in every detail, is to imagine being in a lift or elevator. To be going down may be described as death even before reaching the bottom. It is possible at the last moment to reverse the direction, in which case it may be said that the person has been rescued from Sheol or the gates of death. Once the lift has actually reached the bottom (Sheol) there is no way back (Job 7.9; 10.20–22). All that remains is a shadowy, gloomy existence without meaning or significance and which does not qualify to be called life at all. On the other hand, to be going up in the lift is life, as the traveller is on his way to that fullness of blessing which is found in God's presence. Generally people are somewhere between the top and the bottom, but the really important thing is to be going up (living) and not going down (dying). Proverbs 5.1–6 gives some advice, for instance, on how to avoid the latter. Sickness is another of those influences which draws the lift downwards. Life, the upward movement, may be gained by paying attention to and obeying the word of God (Prov. 4.20–22). The result of this is blessing from God – flocks, riches, prosperity, children (cf. Job 1) – but above all the presence of God himself. To be sure, the Old Testament recognizes that this is not a hard and fast system which applies on every occasion. The book of Job especially tackles the question of what happens when the system fails. The analogy breaks down too because, as Eccles. 1.14–16 recognizes, the same fate overtakes the wise and the foolish. Both in the end die and go to Sheol. The destination of the lift, both up and down, is the same! Those who continue to go up (i.e. live) are eventually 'gathered to their fathers' in Sheol. For the most part in the Old Testament there is no life beyond death. In the New Testament things are somewhat different. The question of the quality of life remains and John 10.10 says that Jesus has come that we might have life 'to the full'. But now there is the further promise of life beyond death.

In the present passage Amos was calling upon the Israelites to press the 'up button' by coming to worship God for his own sake, for the shrines by which they laid so much store would be destroyed. Life depended not on performance of certain forms of worship in certain designated places of worship, helpful as they may be, but on a sincere approach to God himself. Judah would have to learn this truth when Jerusalem would be first threatened (Jer. 7.1–15) and then destroyed (cf. Ezek. 1 and 10). It is a lesson that has to be re-learned (cf. John 4.19ff.), for churches and people go dead when they concentrate on forms and places; they live only when God is central and they seek him for what he is.

Since v. 6 refers to YHWH in the third person it cannot be understood as part of the word from God. It is to be seen as an expansion of it either by Amos himself or by someone else later. It contains a glimmer of hope for if *Joseph's descendants* do *make* their *way to the* LORD they may be spared. If these are Amos' comments he must have been sure, in view of vv. 4 and 5, that the condition would not be fulfilled. In any case the verse ends on a note of judgment with a threat of *fire* (cf. chs. 1–2) to *devour Bethel*. Just as there was *no one to lift up* Samaria in v. 1 so there will be no one to *quench* the fire at Bethel.

Injustice in Israel and Yahweh's judgment

5.7–13   These verses raise some fairly complicated questions. We should note first of all that REB has changed the order of the verses in this section so that the hymn-like passage in vv. 8 and 9 does not interrupt the series of condemnations which seems to begin in v. 7 and continues in vv. 10–12. There is, however, no textual evidence for this. The early versions such as LXX have the same order as the Hebrew text. REB also makes a less obvious change. It obscures the fact that in the Hebrew of vv. 7 and 10 the verbs are in the third person, whereas in vv. 11 and 12 the wrongdoers are addressed directly in the second person. So moving vv. 8–9 does not really solve the problem of continuity between vv. 7 and 10 on the one hand and vv. 11–12 on the other.

Wherever we locate vv. 8–9 there remains the question of their relationship to their context. In the order favoured by REB presumably they reinforce the threat of vv. 4–6, just as 4. 13 reinforced 4. 12, by a reminder of the nature and the power of YHWH. If they come between vv. 7 and 10 as in the Hebrew text we shall need to see them as a parenthetical reminder of the one with whom Israel has to deal.

We are not quite finished with the problems yet, because there are some uncertainties within vv. 8–9. In the first place *the LORD is his name* occurs at the end of v. 8. In the other two hymn-like passages in 4.13 and 9.6 it comes at the end of the passage and not in the middle. Does this perhaps suggest that we should see only v. 8 as the hymn? But then what are we to make of v. 9? Second, v. 8 has to do with natural phenomena such as constellations, dark and light, dry land and sea. Verse 9 however, has to do with YHWH's power to destroy *the mighty* and *the stronghold*. Of course it may be that the hymn included both aspects of YHWH's power. Moreover, it is possible by reading different vowels with the Hebrew consonants to see reference to further constellations (see REB footnote).

In view of all this is it possible to find a coherent interpretation of the passage? Perhaps it is, as follows. Verse 7 begins a new oracle against injustice in Israel. It opens in the Hebrew with what looks like an interrogative particle, but a question would be quite out of place here. Possibly we should read 'Woe to those who . . .' In any case the verse certainly has 'Those who . . .' and goes on to describe how *justice* and *righteousness* (see on 2.6) are not only being disregarded but denied. With 'those who . . .' Amos contrasts *He who* . . . using again as in 4.13 a hymn-like passage ending in *the Lord is his name*, thus sharpening the contrast between Israel and YHWH. Verse 9 may then be seen as a further command by Amos, or even by a later editor, to make clear that YHWH is not only *he who* has power over all the forces of nature but is also he who can overcome all human strength and defences and bring about the destruction he is going on to threaten. Verse 10 then picks up again the description of those mentioned in v. 7, amplifying the rejection of *justice* by the illustration of those who seek to pervert it in the local courts. The Hebrew word behind *court* may be translated as 'gate' and refers to the place where the elders of a town or village or city used to meet, sometimes for conversation and gossip, sometimes to deal with misdemeanours among the inhabitants. Their actions against those who made accusations or bore witness prevented this from happening.

The contrast between Israel and YHWH having been made clear, Amos was now in a position to address the people directly in the second person and to threaten YHWH's judgment on them (vv. 11–12). Although a comparison of REB with, say, RSV will indicate some uncertainty about the meaning of the words translated *levy taxes* and *extort a tribute*, these are almost certainly the correct meanings. The people addressed are obviously the wealthy and powerful who impose heavy demands upon *the poor*, and the threat is that they will not live to enjoy the fruits of their wrong-doing. The *crimes* in v. 12 are the familiar ones again, comparable with those in 2.6. Here again the word *court* is perhaps too formal. It gives an impression of a legal system with judges and barristers in wigs and robes. It refers rather to the much less formal gathering of elders in the gateway who, among other things, dispense justice in their local community. There was some uncertainty about the meaning of *push the humble out of their way* in 2.7. Here the phrase *in court* makes the meaning quite clear. *The destitute* are prevented from obtaining justice from the elders through the bullying and bribery which goes on. Verse 13 offers the final word of judgment. Again, it has that indefiniteness (which we have come to expect in Amos), making it all the more terrifying. *In such a time*, when there is so much wrong and the judgment is to be expected, prudence will dictate that people guilty of such sins should keep quiet. This is probably the correct meaning although *it is prudent* is really a noun, *maśkîl*, and is used in the heading of certain psalms. Psalm 89, for example, is said to be a *maśkîl*. The phrase could just refer to the *maśkîl* or psalm being silent. Either to speak, perhaps calling on God for help, or to sing a psalm to him would be dangerous, for it would only draw attention to the *evil time*.

The two ways

5.14–17 Because vv. 14–15 repeat the call given in vv. 4–6 except that *good* and *evil* have replaced *the LORD* and *Bethel*, some have regarded these two verses as a later comment upon what Amos had said. Against that it may be argued that the idea of the 'Two Ways' is common in writings of the Wisdom tradition such as Prov. 4.18f. and Ps. 1, and we have seen that it is possible that Amos' ways of expressing himself may owe something to Wisdom. On the other hand, in favour of later authorship, we should ask why Amos should want to repeat, in a somewhat more impersonal way, what he had already said in vv. 4–6. The same idea is found in Deuteronomy. Sometimes the language offers a choice between blessing if the people obey and curse if they disobey (Deut. 11.26–28), but in Deut. 30.15, 19 it closely resembles that found here. 'Today I offer you the choice of life and good, or death and evil. . . . Choose life and you and your descendants will live.' Further, Amos offers virtually no opportunity for choice except for the very tentative offer in vv. 4–6 which is very quickly left behind. Deuteronomy, however, clearly sees the possibility of choice leading to life. In Jer. 7.1–15, where there is evidence of Deuteronomic editing, there is a similar discrepancy between the prophet's unconditional message of destruction and the possibility of safety if they 'amend their ways'. On the whole, therefore, it is better to see these two verses as spoken or written by later preachers in the Deuteronomic tradition. The words of Amos in 5.4–6 were used again and the door which Amos had opened there, allowing just a chink of light and hope, was pushed further open as they repeated his message but slightly adapted it according to their beliefs. It should be noted, however, that even if they do *seek good* and *love good* there is no guarantee that *favour* will be shown to them. *It may be that the Lord will show favour.* The final decision rests in the hands of God. A change of heart and mind does not automatically secure a change of fortune. It opens the way for God to *show favour* if he will.

The following verses (16–17) return to the announcement of judgment on Israel. *Those skilled in the dirge* are the 'professional' mourners who may come to sing their laments at times of death and disaster. It is not easy to see what REB means by *and wailing proclaimed to those skilled in the dirge.* Presumably it means that a time of mourning will be proclaimed and *those skilled in the dirge* summoned to take part. The word *proclaimed* is not found in the Hebrew but has been added for the sake of the sense. A better solution to the problem raised by the Hebrew text is to read a very slightly different word instead of *wailing* and so obtain the translation 'He will join with those skilled in mourning', the 'he' being the farmer of the previous line. The passage would then mean that the tragedy about to befall Israel would be so great that the mourning of the 'professionals' would be inadequate and the *farmer* or husbandman would be called in from the fields to supplement their laments. What exactly was this tragedy? As usual Amos went into no details. All YHWH said through him was *I shall pass through your midst.* It was nothing more or less than the presence of God (cf. 4. 12), but that was enough. *Pass through* is not the same word as Passover but it is used in the Passover narrative in Ex. 12. 12 where YHWH promised to 'pass through the land of Egypt and kill every firstborn of man and beast'. Whether or not the audience would have been reminded of this, it does indicate what the *passing through* involves when the people are so much at odds with YHWH.

Three sayings

5.18–27   Three sayings have been placed side by side here, one dealing with *the day of the LORD* (vv. 18–20) and two dealing with worship (vv. 21–24 and 25–27). The first is a word from the prophet himself; the other two are words of YHWH through the prophet although there is no introductory formula to say so, but only the concluding one in v.27.

The first three verses seek to put an end to the high hopes which were associated in people's minds with *the day of the LORD*. Clearly they were looking forward to it because they thought of it as a day of *light*, a word often associated with 'salvation' (cf. Ps. 27.1). The contrast between *darkness* and *light* in this passage is characteristic of much biblical thought and language. It is associated with certain other pairs of opposites, which may be seen within the creation narratives in Gen. 1 and 2, such as order and chaos, dry land and sea (or great deep), cultivated land and desert. The ancient Israelites lived in a world where these dualities were still real. They understood that God was on the side of the positives, but the negatives were always present as a threat which needed to be held in check by God (cf. Ps. 104.7–9). Amos therefore threatened that the negative darkness would overwhelm the positive light, allowed to do so by God, who would normally be expected to reaffirm the positive light on *the day of the Lord* (cf. Isa. 60. 1 and contrast John 1.4–5). Instead of being a day to be anticipated gladly it was one to be avoided. Yet there was no possibility of avoiding it, for judgment was inevitable. To illustrate this Amos drew the famous word-picture of a man *who runs from a lion only to be confronted by a bear*. Escaping into his house he rests with his hand against the wall where a *snake* bites him. So there was no escape for Israel from *the day of the LORD* and its attendant *darkness*. Moreover the darkness was total.

THE DAY OF THE LORD

The question remains about the nature of *the day of the LORD* which the people were expecting and which Amos saw as such a threat. Two main theories have been put forward as to the origin of the idea and the expectation associated with it. First, it may have to do with the great autumn Feast of Tabernacles. The whole Feast was a time of great rejoicing at the gathering in of the fruit harvest, grapes, olives and figs. It also marked the end of the hot, dry summer season and the anticipation of the autumn (or early) rains (cf. Zech. 14. 16–17; also John 7, especially v. 37). The passage in Zech. 14. 16ff. also indicates that YHWH was recognized as King at the Feast. In Canaanite mythology it was Baal who was raised to life, was recognized as King and sent rain. Attempts have been made to reconstruct the Israelite Feast partly on the basis of this, but these need not concern us now. It is enough to know that YHWH was King and provider of rain and fertility. His kingship further implied victory for his people over other nations and the superiority of Israel (Pss. 96 and 98). Deut. 31.10 tells us that every seven years the law was read at this Feast, and the law is sometimes described as light (Ps. 119.105; Isa. 2.5). If John 8 was also spoken on the same occasion as John 7 then this shows an association of light with the Feast of Tabernacles. Year after year the hopes of Israel's subjection of other nations and the recognition of their God as King remained unfulfilled and so became projected into a more distant future day. Since the following two passages have to do with worship it is possible that all this underlies Amos' use of the phrase.

Second, it is suggested that *the day of the LORD* may have at its heart the belief that all Israel's victories in the past had been achieved not by her armies but by YHWH. Indeed it was his war. He had defeated Pharaoh and brought them out of Egypt without any effort on their part (Ex. 14.14), he had brought them into Canaan, delivering Jericho into their hands without a battle (Josh. 6.8); he had defeated the Philistines using only a young shepherd's sling (I Sam. 17). *The day of the LORD*, then, is the day when he will grant them ultimate victory over all their foes. This is why the day is often associated with military imagery. Isaiah had to stand this hope on its head by saying that YHWH would fight against his people and this would be 'a strange deed, an alien task' (28.21). Amos had already made a similar point (cf. 3.2 and 4.12).

It is not really necessary to decide whether Amos had one or the other of these views in mind. They have sufficient in common to indicate why people looked forward to *the day*. It need not have been in any sense a technical term but just a phrase for the coming day when YHWH would do great things for Israel and its associations may have been many and varied. Amos's rejection of all its positive associations is beyond doubt and there is no passage in the whole book which speaks so clearly of Israel's total destruction.

5.21–24   take up again the theme of YHWH's rejection of all their worship in the words of YHWH himself. Since he refers to *pilgrim-feasts* we should probably be right in thinking of Bethel again. The fact that he does not mention the shrine indicates that here at least it is not the place of worship which is being condemned; it is not the fact that Bethel is a schismatic shrine. Both 4.4 and 5.4 have dealt with Israel's cultic activity, and there it was argued that the chief complaint was that YHWH was being ignored in favour of the festivals and rites for their own sake. Here the complaint is different and we must beware of thinking that Amos criticized Israel's worship always for the same reason. It is useful in this context to compare passages in the other prophets on the same subject, e.g. Isa. 1.10ff.; Jer. 6.20; 7.24; Hos. 6.6; Micah 6.6f. In some cases there appears to be a criticism of worship as currently practised, as in the present passage. In others there seems to be an outright rejection of organized worship altogether, as in the following passage vv. 25–27. In each case we have to decide what the prophet meant when he spoke to his own people.

YHWH's rejection of Israel's sacrificial worship in vv. 21–24 is expressed in extremely strong terms. He 'hates' and 'rejects' it. The *pilgrim-feasts* were the three main feasts in Israel, Unleavened Bread, Weeks and Tabernacles. All of them were harvest feasts, the first two of grain and the last of fruit, but all of them came to be associated with moments in Israel's history, the exodus from Egypt, the giving of the law at Sinai, and the dwelling in 'booths' in the wilderness (Ex. 23.14–17; 34.18–24; Lev. 23.4–44; Deut. 16.1–17). All Israelite males were to 'go up' to the sanctuary on these occasions and for most Northern Israelites this would be Bethel. The Feast of Tabernacles became the most important of the three and could sometimes be referred to as 'the Feast'. I Kings 12. 32 tells us that Jeroboam I instituted this Feast at Bethel a month later than the traditional date of its celebration in Jerusalem. Some think that by using the plural here Amos was referring to successive Feasts of Tabernacles but he may well not have been as precise as that. *Pilgrim-feasts* in general are more likely.

The *whole-offerings* of v. 22 were burned on the altar in their entirety once the blood had been drained off. They were offered as an act of homage to God. The *grain-offerings* had a similar purpose and sometimes accompanied the whole-offering. Not all of it was burned though; some was reserved for the priests. The *shared-offerings* are sometimes known as 'peace offerings' because their name is derived from the Hebrew noun frequently translated 'peace' (*shalom*). The purpose of the offering is to be deduced more from the practice of it than the name. After the blood had been drained off, certain parts were burnt on the altar and the rest was shared and eaten by priests and people. The idea seems to be to maintain relationships through a shared meal (see Lev. 1–7). Amos, however, makes nothing of the distinction between them and is more concerned to condemn sacrifice as a whole. It should be noted that none of these three sacrifices is said to deal with sin by being the means through which divine forgiveness is offered. The two sacrifices specifically meant for this purpose were the 'sin-offering' and the 'guilt-offering'. Therefore it is not the issue of forgiveness which is at stake here any more than it was in 4.4f. Acts of homage and the sharing of meat before God were offensive to him. The laws governing these offerings may be found in Lev. 1–7, and although they may have been codified later they were quite probably in force in Amos' time. But it was not wrong practice which Amos condemned. It was the fact that they offered sacrifices at all. The *songs* they sang in worship to the accompaniment of *lutes* were equally offensive to him.

The reason is stated in v. 24, or at least the way to make them acceptable is made clear. They would have to be accompanied by *justice* and *righteousness* and the assumption is that these are lacking in Israel. This has been Amos' complaint all along. The *torrent* is the stream that flows from the hills in flood when the rains come but dries up during the hot, dry summer. This reference to water may be a link with the Feast of Tabernacles and *the day of the* LORD as described above. *Justice* and *righteousness* (see on 1.6) must not be things of fits and starts. They must be a consistent feature of the nation's life if its corporate and organized worship is to be pleasing to God so maintaining a proper relationship with him.

5.25–27 raise some interesting questions and v. 26 in particular presents some very serious problems of translation and interpretation. Verse 25 seems to suggest that sacrifices are not necessary at all, for the question asked clearly demands the answer 'No': their ancestors did not offer sacrifices in the wilderness and therefore there is no need for them to do so now. Is it true that no sacrifices were offered during the time of the wilderness wanderings following the exodus? If we look carefully at the record we possess in the books of Exodus and Numbers it is not strictly true, although sacrifice is not frequently said to have been offered. It could be argued that Passover was celebrated, but that was hardly a sacrifice of the kind intended here. It was not a pilgrim-feast, but was celebrated in the tents or homes as a reminder of God's deliverance. Indeed in the nature of things there could not be any *pilgrim-feasts* for there was no settled sanctuary for them to visit. Ex. 24 describes a covenant ceremony at Sinai but all this amounts to very little and Amos was virtually correct. Jeremiah makes exactly the same point (7.21). There are many scholars who would argue that Israel's sacrificial system developed only after the entry into Canaan and largely under Canaanite influence, though this may be going too far. So is Amos arguing that sacrifice is not necessary? If we understand the word 'necessary' in its strict sense he probably is. Sacrifice was not essential; people had got along without it before and might do so again. But it is hard to imagine that Amos believed sacrifice to be undesirable. Properly offered, that is, offered as a true act of homage to God and by people who sought to maintain standards of behaviour consonant with their calling as the people of God, sacrifice was acceptable to God and he was pleased to receive it.

All this assumes that these two verses (25–26) were actually spoken by Amos, but, as we noted in 2.10, the pre-exilic prophets do not mention the forty years' duration of the wilderness wandering. Moreover, not only is v. 25 similar in meaning to Jer. 7.21 but it seems more appropriate to the late seventh century when Judah was destined to face again a period when sacrifice would not be possible for the Babylonian exiles since by then it could be offered only in the Jerusalem Temple.

The peculiarities of v. 26 again cast some doubt upon authorship. In any case there is certainly a time gap and a history of interpretation between the words spoken and the form of the verse as we now have it. It is just possible that it continues the question of v. 25 about what Israel did or did not do during the wilderness wanderings 'And did you take up . . . ?' The most natural meaning of the Hebrew, however, suggests that this verse is looking to the future as in REB. Then the question arises as to what they *will take up* as they are driven into exile. Here it is necessary to mention some Hebrew words. The two things they will *take up* according to the Hebrew Bible are *sikkût* (REB **shrine**) and *kiyyûn* (REB *pedestals*). It is important to remember that the earliest manuscripts were written using consonants only. From this consonantal text the Rabbis were able to read as they went along, just as we should be able to read 'Th Lrd s m shphrd'. Later, vowel signs were added to the consonants to indicate more clearly what words should be read. Now it will be noticed that the two words mentioned above both have the same vowel pattern, *i-û*. This is because when the Rabbis came to a word which was too abhorrent to be spoken, such as the name of a foreign god, they often replaced it with the word *šiqqûs* which means 'abomination'. When vowels were added to the manuscript the vowels of this word which was read were supplied to the consonants which were written, producing a 'hybrid' form. If, in this case, we look only at the consonants we find *skkt* (which can mean 'booth' or 'shelter') and *kyyn* (which can mean 'pedestal'), and this is what REB has translated. These words, however, would not be so abhorrent to the Rabbis that they refused to read them, and so it is now thought that at some time before vowel signs were added to the manuscript in the seventh century CE these two words had come to be understood as the names of foreign gods, Sakkuth and Kaiwan (see RSV and REB footnote) The Septuagint (Greek) also understood them in this way. The Vulgate (Latin) and Targum (Aramaic) have words meaning 'shelter' and 'pedestal', and so REB has every reason to translate as it does in the text rather than in the footnote, except that the word *sukkat* means 'shelter' rather than *shrine* and there is no Hebrew word corresponding to *idol*. The phrase simply means 'booth (shelter) of your King' or perhaps 'your royal booth'. The great Feast of Tabernacles is called the feast of *Sukkoth* (shelters, booths). It may be that the verse means that the 'booth' used by the king at the Feast of the Tabernacles was to be carried away along with the pedestal for their images. This, if from Amos, might possibly refer to the bull at Bethel, which was originally seen as a pedestal or throne for YHWH but was later regarded as an idol (cf. Hos. 8.5). There are two other words in the Hebrew which have been omitted by REB and relegated to a footnote – 'the star of your God'. This is usually taken to mean 'your star gods' and thought to be a later addition by the Rabbis to describe the gods Sakkut and Kaiwan, whose names they thought stood in the text before them.

J. H. Hayes[1] has pointed out, however, that 'star' may not refer to the heavenly body at all but to a star on the standard or ensign carried by the king. In Num. 24.17 the word is in parallel with 'sceptre' and so there is much to be said for this view. Perhaps, therefore, either Amos or the later author of these verses was saying that there were three objects to be carried away, all used at the Festival of Booths; the royal booth, the pedestal for God or gods, and the star ensign, the symbol of divinity. All these, however, were man-made and transient. In so far as they had come to be regarded not just as symbols but as objects of veneration and worship they would be carried away with the people. The threat of *exile beyond Damascus* is more specific than Amos' usual threats and again may point to the seventh rather than to the eighth century. On the other hand some punishment is to be expected after vv. 21–24. Perhaps the most likely view is that Amos' original threat has been overlaid with seventh-century concepts when his words were used later. This uncertainty should not be allowed to detract from the message of this whole section. *The day of the* LORD is a time to anticipate not with joy but with fear because worship offered without just behaviour in everyday social life is offensive to God and the opportunity to offer it will be removed.

Although chapter 6 contains several sayings of Amos which may originally have been spoken on different occasions, they are now put together to produce a more or less coherent whole.

Against the nobility

6.1–7.   Like the beginning of chapter 4, this section deals with the excesses of the nobility in Samaria, though it does not pick out the womenfolk for special attention. The major difference is that, as it now stands, this addresses the people of *Zion* in the Southern Kingdom of Judah as well as the Northern king's court in *Samaria*. Some would argue that Amos, being a Judaean himself, was quite capable of criticizing the life-style at court in both kingdoms. This, of

[1] Hayes, *Amos*, p. 178.

course, is true and he may indeed have had one eye on his own country while attacking the neighbouring one. Moreover the people of Samaria might well have applauded his comment about Zion and so have been even more surprised and angry when, in the second line, he accused them of similar behaviour. Others, however, regard the presence of *Zion* as further evidence for the later use of Amos' words in Judah and believe that the word originally used by Amos was 'Bethel'. There may be some support for this in the fact that *Zion* is used and not Jerusalem, for *Zion* often denotes the religious aspect of the Southern capital and 'Jerusalem' its more political aspect. Therefore 'Jerusalem' would have been the more natural parallel with Samaria. If, however, 'Bethel' had originally stood here, then, since it was the religious royal town of the North it would have been natural to substitute the Southern religious equivalent. Neither argument is conclusive and we can only say that the words we now possess in the book condemn complacency among leaders wherever it may be found.

The Hebrew of the last two lines of the first verse is difficult to translate and understand. As translated by REB the *men of mark* are the leaders of Israel, *the first of nations* is Israel itself. In what sense the ordinary *people of Israel have recourse* to them is not wholly clear, perhaps for advice or assistance. The noun translated *men of mark* is not found elsewhere in the Old Testament. The verb from which it is derived usually means 'to pierce' or 'bore'. One part of the verb does signify 'picked out' and a similar Arabic word means 'leader' or 'chief' and REB has followed this line. *First of nations* is an unusual phrase. Nowhere else is it used of Israel and if Amos used it in that sense he must have been doing so sarcastically. It is used in Num. 24.20 of the Amalekites, in the sense that they were the earliest nation, and in Deut. 11.41, where it refers to the chief part of the Ammonites. The last line of the verse reads literally 'they come to them, house of Israel' or possibly 'the house of Israel come to them' but the verb is plural. A slight change of one letter would allow us to translate:

> Go round to the first of nations
> Come to them, house of Israel.

This would mean that the invitation to visit and examine what is the situation elsewhere begins in the second half of v. 1 and continues in v. 2. Exactly what it is about *Calneh, Hamath* and *Gath* that they are invited to look at is unclear. If the words are from Amos (c. 750 BCE) they cannot refer to their destruction, for Calneh and Hamath were not destroyed until 738 while Gath lost its independence in 734 and was destroyed in 711 BCE. It could be an invitation to see them on the verge of destruction but the dates still make that unlikely. Or it could be an invitation to see that the complacency in Israel is simply a reflection of that found elsewhere and therefore that Samaria is no better than the cities in other nations. This last interpretation is more likely if we read the double question which follows as offering real alternative assessments of the situation. This is possible because there are no pronouns in the first half of the question in Hebrew. They have to be supplied, and probably we should supply 'you', not *they:*

> Are you better than these kingdoms
> Or is their territory greater than yours?

So Amos' audience is asked to examine the evidence and decide whether Israel has anything special going for it. In 1.2–26 he had claimed that Israel was on the same footing as the other nations. In 9. 7–8 he will claim that other nations were guided by YHWH as well as Israel. Israel's status as the chosen people can no longer provide them with any advantage, for they show the same kind of arrogance and complacency as other people round about.

The following vv. 3–6 may refer to any feasting at the court, but v. 3 probably suggests a more particular reference to the Feast of Tabernacles. *You thrust aside all thought of* represents one Hebrew word which normally means 'to spurn' as in Isa. 66.5. By substituting one consonant for a very similar one with which it can very easily be confused in reading we could translate 'You announce the day of evil' and this word 'announce' is used in parallel with *hasten* or 'bring near' in, for instance, Isa. 41.22; 45.21. What they should announce, of course, is the 'day of YHWH'. What they should bring near or *hasten* is the *reign* or enthronement of YHWH. Amos had already described their anticipation of *the day of the LORD* (5.18ff.) and shown it to be folly. The day was one of *darkness, not light.* Ironically, therefore, he can speak of the 'day of YHWH' as the 'day of evil' and of the enthronement of YHWH which was a feature of the Feast of Tabernacles, as the enthronement of violence. In Samaria *evil* and *violence* have replaced YHWH and so their celebration is fatally flawed.

A description of the feasting follows in vv. 4–6 and reveals their luxurious way of life when they were supposed to be offering worship to God. *Lambs from the flock* probably represent the best quality (I Sam. 15.9) and used in sacrifice (Ezek. 39.18). The same applied to *stall-fed calves* (cf. I Sam. 28.24, where REB translates a similar phrase 'fattened calf'). *Like David*, if original, indicates their inflated opinion of themselves as musicians. In the midst of all this the impending destruction of the kingdom does not make them *feel grief*. This word really means 'become sick or ill' and it may be used deliberately to suggest that, though they become sick through all their feasting, the fate of *Joseph* (the Northern Kingdom) leaves them unaffected because they never think about it.

The judgment in v. 7 is slightly more precise than we have been used to in Amos. It involves deportation or *exile*. The word translated *laughter* occurs only here and in Jer. 16.5, where it means a funeral feast. It had this meaning also in the Aramaic. Moreover there is no connecting word *and* in the Hebrew so that the line actually says 'And the funeral feast of the loungers will depart'. By this he means that the feast which they have been enjoying will come to an end and will be seen to have been a 'funeral feast' instead of a joyous one since *evil* and *violence* have been crowned instead of YHWH.

Samaria's destruction

6.8–11 As in 4.2 this further threat is introduced by an oath validated by YHWH *himself*. *The arrogance of Jacob* refers to the attitude of the people described in the previous verses who thought they could ignore God and behave just as they liked. However, the phrase could be translated 'pride of Jacob' meaning that of which the people were proud, i.e. Samaria itself. Such an interpretation would be supported by the references to *palaces* in the parallel line and *the city* in the last line.

The difficulties in v. 10 are many and varied. It may be useful to list them before attempting an interpretation. First, the Hebrew word translated *relative* usually means 'lover' or 'darling' and that is inappropriate here. On the basis of Lev. 10.4 it may mean 'uncle', probably on the father's side. REB has preferred not to be quite as precise. Second, *embalmer* represents a Hebrew word which means 'one who burns him (or it)'. The Israelites did not normally cremate their dead and if this were what Amos intended here we should have to say that there were some special reasons for doing so. Some have thought the deaths were due to plague, though there is nothing to say so. In view of the military background it is possible to argue that the bodies had lain there some time and their condition required them to be burned (cf. 4.10). It has also been suggested that the term refers to 'one who burns (incense) for him (it)'. Yet another suggestion, almost too good to be true, is that the word is derived from a verb with a quite different meaning and refers to a kinsman on the mother's side of the family. Third, we cannot be sure whether these two words, *relative* and *embalmer*, refer to the same person or to two different ones. Fourth, the word translated *body* literally means 'bones' and we cannot be sure whether it refers to one corpse or to all ten. Fifth, we do not know who is meant by *someone in a corner of the house*, though presumably it is one who has gone in to investigate. Sixth, if we are right in thinking of the *ten* as a military unit, the *house* would not be a domestic dwelling, but living quarters for those soldiers. The word could easily mean that. Seventh, why does the person outside say *hush*, and who adds *the name of the Lord must not be mentioned* and why?

It looks, then, as though Amos was drawing a picture of what was to happen when the Northern Kingdom, and Samaria in particular, was finally overrun.

It seems as though the small army unit had retreated to its quarters, but had been pursued and its soldiers killed there. Relatives or friends began to search the premises for survivors, one standing outside and the other going in to the farthest corners. The one outside enquired about survivors but none could be found and, in the presence of such a calamity, only silence was appropriate (cf. 5.13). Either Amos himself (see REB) or the person waiting outside added the reason – that it would be unwise, unsafe to speak the divine name, probably because that would be to invoke YHWH's presence and his presence in such a situation as Israel was in would only bring more disaster.

Such a picture, so vividly painted, was Amos' way of portraying the divine judgment which he foresaw for Israel.

6.11   is either a poetic oracle to round off the prose passage or an originally separate oracle placed here because of the reference to *houses*. In any case it now functions as a further threat that all *houses*, both *great* and *small* will be smashed to pieces.

The perversion of justice and Yahweh's response

6.12–14   This short section begins with two rhetorical questions in the style of Wisdom teaching (cf. 3.3–8). The folly involved in the two activities is obvious enough. Equally foolish, and they should have known better, was the Israelites' perversion of justice, *the process of law*, and 'righteousness', *justice itself* (see on 1.6).

In v. 13, as the REB footnote indicates, there is a play on the names of two towns, Lo-debar, which means *nothing* and Karnaim which means 'horns'. These latter are frequently a symbol of *power*. References to a town called Lo-debar in II Sam. 9.4, 5 and 17.27 indicate that it was situated somewhere in Trans-jordania, probably in Gilead. Karnaim is mentioned only in Gen. 14.5 (possibly) and in I Macc. 5.43, 44; II Macc. 12.12, where it is in roughly the same area. It is probably best to follow the hint given in the footnote and understand Amos as speaking about the recent capture of these two towns. Otherwise it is difficult to see what *'Jubilant over a nothing'* means and it is doubtful whether the pronouncing of two ordinary words would have called to people's mind two little known towns. It has to be admitted, however, that the various early translations in Greek and Syriac do not have names of the towns. If Amos did name them, we should have to assume that Jeroboam had recaptured them from someone else earlier in his reign, and that the people were now claiming all the credit for it themselves without any recognition of YHWH's part in it. The consequences of these actions and attitudes would be that the YHWH, whose help they failed to recognize, would now send *a nation* to *harry* or oppress the whole territory over which Jeroboam II ruled, defined by *Lebo-hamath* in the north and the *wadi of the Arabah* to the south (cf. II Kings 14.25–28 and Introduction, p.5). Who the nation would be Amos, typically, does not specify; nor, in a sense, does it matter, for it is YHWH with whom Israel has to deal and *a nation* is no more than his instrument. When, some years later, the Assyrian threat was closer to Judah, Isaiah could use similar language (Isa. 10.5ff.).

Visions foretelling doom upon Israel
Amos 7.1–9.8*a*

This long section needs to be considered as a whole. So far, for the most part, we have been dealing with prophetic oracles in a poetic style. Now we find a passage in descriptive prose, telling of four visions interspersed by a narrative in which Amos' authority as a prophet was questioned by the priest at Bethel. There is a fifth vision in 9.1–4 and some prefer to see all five as belonging to the series. The fifth, however, although similar in form, does seem different in character and, in any case, it is so far separated from these four that it is best dealt with later. These four have sometimes been regarded as call visions which Amos saw while still at work on his sheep farm. Their position in the middle of the book is then explained as part of the editorial process. We are reminded that the description of Isaiah's call does not appear until ch. 6, but it is possible to explain that by claiming that the present book of Isaiah is made up of several earlier and smaller collections of which chs. 6–9 is one. There is no evidence of earlier collections here in Amos and there seems to be no reason why a prophet should not see visions during the course of his ministry as well as, or instead of at the beginning. Moreover, when we read the account of them there is nothing to suggest the commissioning of Amos as a prophet. Indeed, in the first two he already makes intercession for Israel and this may be seen as a part of the prophetic role. What they do, in fact, is to set out clearly the message which Amos must deliver to Israel, and they may well have come to him not in quick succession but over a period of time, for in spite of their similarity they do exhibit differences which indicate some development of the message. It was indicated in the introduction (1. 1) that this was the way he received his message in visions. It is usual to describe these as visions but that does not necessarily imply that the things he saw were only in his imagination. Certainly in some cases it implies a heightened sense of the significance of ordinary things which he actually saw. The first two visions are what might be called 'event' visions in which the prophet 'saw' certain natural phenomena taking place and recognized in them a deeper meaning than appeared on the surface. The second pair may be called 'object' visions in which the prophet saw certain objects the names of which brought to mind other words which formed the basis of what he had to say. The first pair leave the door open for intercession and possible salvation in response to it. The first contains a prayer that God will change his mind, the second a prayer that he will cease from what he is doing, the third and fourth contain no intercession at all, presumably because it is too late (cf. Jer. 11.14, where the prophet is told not to pray). If the visions came to him over a period of time, it suggests that early on Amos had not given up hope for Israel, but that it was gradually borne in upon him that there was no hope and no future for the nation.

It is obvious, but perhaps needs to be said, that they are private visions in which only the prophet's consciousness is involved. No one else could be aware of what Amos had 'seen' in the events or objects. We are bound to assume, therefore, that Amos found it necessary to recount them to others at some point, though we can only guess why or when. We have already seen that his authority was probably challenged by his audience (cf. 3.2–8) and he may well have told of his visions in order to justify his message of darkness and destruction. This would then explain or suggest a reason for the insertion of the passage in 7.10–17 between the third and fourth visions, for this also deals with the question of Amos' authority. It is sometimes suggested that this insertion was prompted by the final threat in the third vision, a threat against the king. It is true that this is picked up in the Amaziah episode but it is not the fundamental question, and the relationship between vv. 10–17 and the visions goes deeper than a mere verbal link. It is the question of Amos' authority which provides the inner unity of the whole section. We must now look at each vision in detail, remembering that in the form in which we now possess them they are carefully constructed and crafted literary accounts.

The first vision: Locusts

7.1–3 The first vision was of *a swarm of locusts*. Such plagues were not unfamiliar, as is suggested by the list of different kinds of locusts in Joel 1.4. Whether Amos actually saw such a *swarm* we have no means of knowing. He may have done or it may have been purely visionary. In either case the emphasis in the Hebrew text is on the one 'assembling' the *swarm*. This is obscured by REB's translation, which follows the Septuagint translation and requires a change of vowels in the Hebrew. In fact the vision begins, as do the second and third visions, with a participle without a subject, and should be translated 'Look! Someone assembling a swarm of locusts.' The 'someone' is of course YHWH, as Amos well knew and as the people around would recognize too, but the withholding of the name adds a sense of mystery to the vision. The locusts' attack was on *the later corn* which should have been available to the ordinary farmer and his people. It is not certain that we should think of two separate harvests, one for the use of the royal court and the second for more general use. In view of what was said in the Introduction (p.6) and on 2. 8, it probably means that the first corn cut had to be delivered to the royal landlords for use at court. After that the remainder of the harvest was available to the farmer. What is under threat is the people's food supply. Before this could be reaped the locusts had moved in. They had just about *devoured every trace of vegetation in the land* when Amos intervened on behalf of the people and begged forgiveness. Amos had spoken of the nation as the descendants of Jacob (3.13), and of Samaria as the pride of Jacob (6.8) but he had preferred 'Israel' when speaking of the contemporary people. Here he uses Jacob, and we must wonder whether this is deliberate. Was it because his visions were recounted at Bethel, where Jacob had his dream and which became associated with the patriarch thereafter (Gen. 28)? Or was it meant to recall sinful Jacob before his name was changed to Israel (cf. Gen. 32.28 and Hos. 12.2–5)? We have no means of knowing. What we can say is that the appeal for forgiveness was not made on the grounds that Israel or Jacob was important, nor on the grounds that they were the chosen people. It was on the grounds that *Jacob* was *small*, which probably refers not to the size of the country but to its insignificance. The word translated *How* very rarely means that and is more likely to be an abbreviated form of the 'wish' formula as found also in several places in the Old Testament (e.g.

Num. 11.4, 'If only . . .'; II Sam. 15.4 etc.). The plea then is 'If only Jacob could stand (*survive*)! He is so insignificant.' The prayer for forgiveness is not and cannot be based on human achievement, but only on the mercy of God towards those who recognize their frailty. The prayer is answered (v. 3) not with an explicit promise of forgiveness though it is probably implied in that YHWH *relented*, i.e. was moved to pity and promised that such a devastation would *not* *happen*.

The second vision: Drought

7. 4–6   The second vision carried with it a threat of drought. The footnote in REB hints at some problems with the translation *The Lord GOD was summoning a flame of fire*. In the first place the words *Lord God* come at a very awkward point in the Hebrew sentence and certainly not where the subject of *summoning* would normally come. As was indicated in 7.1, it is better to see these words as a later clarification of who was doing the summoning and to regard the subject in Amos' original saying as an indefinite 'someone'. Second, what is actually being summoned? *Flame of fire* involves some slight alterations to the Hebrew text which have no support in the Septuagint translation. The Hebrew says either 'to contend' or 'for a contention', the infinitive and the noun having the same form. The noun means a 'quarrel' or 'dispute' and is often used of a legal dispute. Hayes[1] thinks it refers to a quarrel or war and that the mythological language which follows is metaphorical. This supports the general thesis of his commentary that Israel was on the verge of civil war, but it appears to be stretching the language too much. More likely, it means that 'someone', and it must be YHWH as now expressed, is in conflict with Israel. The fire is then the instrument he used to pursue the conflict. The problem then arises that although you can summon *a flame of fire* you cannot 'summon a contention or dispute'. The verb may, however, be translated 'proclaim' and that certainly eases the sense 'someone' proclaiming a quarrel by fire. We have already met the idea of YHWH attacking Israel with fire in 5.6. The meaning here is slightly different,

[1] Hayes, *Amos*, p.203.

for *the great abyss* is the underground sea upon which the Israelites thought the world was founded (Pss. 24.2; 104.5). In Gen. 1, 'the deep' was divided at creation into the waters above and those below the vault or firmament of heaven. The waters above came through the vault as rain when God 'opened the windows of heaven', and when 'the springs of the great deep burst out' there was a flood (Gen. 7.11–12). For the *fire to devour the great abyss* was therefore to dry up the underground waters which fed the springs and rivers and so to threaten the water supply without which *the land* also would be scorched and return to desert (cf. Gen. 2.5–6). This time Amos prayed not for forgiveness but simply that God would stop doing this and call off his quarrel. The grounds for his prayer were exactly the same and so was the result.

The third vision: a Plumb-line?

7.7–9 The third vision concerned not an event but an object and in almost all English translations the object is *a plumb-line*. If this is the meaning of the word then the message is fairly clear. Again, 'someone' *was standing by a wall (built with the aid) of a plumb-line* – the words in brackets have to be added to make sense – with *a plumb-line in his hand*. This may well have been something that Amos actually and literally saw. It is the *plumb-line* which catches his attention and brings to mind the message that YHWH will set *a plumb-line in the midst of my people, Israel* and, unlike the wall, Israel will be found to be out of true. This is what YHWH said to him through the vision. Before he had time to make intercession YHWH continued with the threat that *never again* would he *pardon them*. The word translated *plumb-line* is used only here and may have been chosen because of its similarity in sound to two other Hebrew words which mean 'to moan' or 'to groan'. In this case there is an implicit word play whereas in the fourth vision it is explicit.

Before commenting on v. 9 we need to look more closely at this word *plumb-line*. As has been said, the Hebrew word used here occurs nowhere else in Hebrew literature and so there is no other context by which we may check its meaning. On the basis of similar words in other languages it is generally agreed that it refers to a metal of some kind and most think of it as lead. The *wall* in the present passage would then be a 'wall of lead'. This has seemed strange and so 'lead' has been interpreted as the lead bob at the end of a *plumb-line*. The *wall* then becomes the 'wall of a plumb-line', which does not make much better sense and has therefore been further interpreted to mean a *wall built with the aid of a plumb-line*. By now we have moved quite a few steps away from the literal meaning. It can be seen that this is a somewhat dubious line of reasoning and so some commentators prefer to omit the word *plumb-line* altogether where it first occurs with the wall, regarding it as a copyist's error. Of course they have retained *plumb-line* in the rest of the passage, where it occurs three more times. If, however, the meaning *plumb-line* is so uncertain then this makes the exegesis of the whole vision uncertain. More recently A. G. Auld[2] has taken up an argument used by H. Gese[3] that on the basis of other languages the word really means 'tin' and not 'lead', in which case the idea of a *plumb-line* disappears altogether. The Septuagint calls it a 'wall of adamantus', that is, a hard metal of some kind. It may be argued that tin is not a hard metal but then neither is lead! However, 'someone standing by a tin wall with tin in his hand' still remains a strange vision. It should be said that 'a tin wall' does not mean a wall made exclusively of tin any more than 'ivory houses' (3.15) means houses made of ivory. REB was right to translate this as houses adorned with ivory, and the phrase in this verse simply means 'a wall reinforced by or decorated with tin'. There are then three ways of understanding the vision. First, since tin is a constituent of bronze, which was used for arms in the ancient world, Auld[4] and Hayes [5] see the metal wall as a symbol of unconquerability advancing against Israel and the LORD standing by with more in his hand, i.e. further reserves of arms with which to attack Israel. The vision is therefore a threat of attack which is irresistible. This is an attractive interpretation except that the idea of a wall as an offensive weapon is unusual. So, second, the metal wall was a defensive wall which Israel had erected and the builder was standing beside it with more metal in his hand to strengthen it still further. It was in this sense that Jeremiah was described as 'an iron pillar, a bronze wall' which

[2] Auld, *Amos*, pp. 18f.
[3] H. Gese, 'Composition bei Amos', *Supplement to Vetus Testamentum* 34 (Congress Volume, Vienna 1980), Leyden 1981, pp. 74–95.
[4] Auld, loc. cit.
[5] Hayes, *Amos*, p. 205.

his enemies would be unable to break down (Jer. 1.18). In the present passage the metal wall stood for everything that Israel relied on for security and which led to the kind of complacency described in 6.1. YHWH, however, was bringing more 'tin', i.e. armaments, against Israel to destroy the people and their sanctuaries. A third view takes its cue from the fourth vision, where Amos' attention was directed to the *ripe summer fruit* and the *basket* was of no significance. So here his attention was caught by the 'tin' and the wall was not a significant part of the vision. In both cases Amos actually saw things which became meaningful because their names brought to mind other words with a different and threatening meaning. The fact that the 'tin' is mentioned four times and the wall only once reinforces this view. Amos saw someone decorating a wall, any wall, possibly even a house wall, with tin. The word for 'tin' (*ănāk*) reminded him not only of arms but also of the words for 'moan' (*'ānaḥ*) and 'groan' (*'ānaq*), which are almost identical in sound, and so he saw the tin as a threat that YHWH was about to attack Israel and so cause great distress to the people. This third view has the virtue of being simpler and more straightforward.

This time YHWH refused forgiveness before it could be sought and threatened that *the shrines of Isaac . . . and the sanctuaries of Israel* would be destroyed. The mention of *Isaac* is a little strange since the shrines with which he was associated were in the south. Beersheba, however, is mentioned in 5.5, where there were some grounds for regarding it as a southern addition. Could *Isaac* have replaced an earlier 'Jacob' here for a similar reason? *The house of Jeroboam* in v. 9 is usually taken to mean the royal dynasty. It certainly was by the editor of the book, for it is said to be the reason for the altercation between Amos and Amaziah which follows in vv. 10–17. It is possible, though, that it is parallel with 'shrine' and 'sanctuary' and is a sarcastic reference to Bethel. Beth-el, the house of God, has become Beth-Jeroboam, the house of Jeroboam. If this is so there is no need to regard this last phrase as an editorial addition as many commentators do.

This third vision, then, informs Amos that YHWH is about to attack Israel. The shrines will be destroyed (cf. 5.5) and, perhaps, the royal house will be brought down.

Authority over Bethel

7.10–17 The question usually raised in connection with this famous passage is whether Amos was a 'prophet' since in v. 14 he seems to deny that he was, or is. This is probably to begin with the wrong question. The real theme of the passage is: who has authority over the shrine at Bethel?

First of all we must begin by stating the obvious, although it is sometimes overlooked. The account is not given by Amos; it is about a confrontation between Amos and Amaziah and is recorded by someone else. Who recorded it we do not and cannot know. On the whole the prophetic books show minimal interest in the life and experience of the prophets; they are much more concerned with their words, and so it is unlikely that the story was included just to tell readers about an incident in Amos' life. It has been included as a contribution to a discussion about the authority of different groups of people, prophet, priest and king and, above all, the authority of YHWH. Such discussions may be seen elsewhere and they took the form of narrative. The conflict between Jeremiah and Hananiah in Jer. 27 and 28 is another example of this genre, discussing the problem of true and false prophecy. This is not to say that the event never happened but the main interest of the narrator is not in the historicity of the incident but in the theological questions raised.

This question of authority had been raised by the apparent disclosure by Amos of the visions he had received and particularly the third vision which ended with the threat against *the house of Jeroboam*, which may, as we have seen, carry suggestions of both the royal house and the royal shrine. He had also made strong attacks on the worship being offered there (4.4; 5.4; 5.21). So in the narrative Amaziah accuses him of conspiring against Jeroboam, understanding *the house of Jeroboam* to mean the royal house. Such a conspiracy had to be taken seriously in Israel because prophets had been involved in coups against the existing dynasty (cf. I Kings 19.15–18; 22.1–38). But the narrator probably had in mind also that the other Jeroboam, Jeroboam I, had been anointed king over Northern Israel by Ahijah the prophet even before Solomon had died. Now, thought Amaziah, his namesake Jeroboam II would be brought to an end by Amos the prophet. He addressed Amos directly, acknowledging him as a *seer*. This is a noun not in frequent use in the Old Testament, occurring only sixteen times altogether, nine of them in the book of Chronicles.

In I Sam. 9.9 it is said 'For what is nowadays called a prophet used to be called a seer,' indicating either a simple change of name or the identification of one role with another. D. L. Petersen[6] has suggested that *seer* was a Judaean term for what Israelites would have called a 'prophet' and that by using the term here Amaziah was recognizing Amos' authority in Judah but not in Israel. Be that as it may, his main point is valid, i.e., that Amos' authority in Israel is at the heart of the matter. The Hebrew of v. 12 lays greater emphasis on the *there* than the REB suggests. Amos is to go home to Judah *there* to *earn* his *living* and *there* to *do* his *prophesying*. The challenge is not to his status as a prophet but to his claim to have authority to prophesy in Israel and at Bethel. It is Amaziah himself who has authority there, holding it, as priest, under the ultimate authority of the king, for it is *a royal shrine*.

Amos' reply is a curious one and it is v. 14 which has been the cause of so much discussion and a multitude of learned articles. The most natural translation of the Hebrew would be 'I *am* not a prophet . . .'. Hebrew, like many languages, can often omit the verb 'to be' from a sentence, leaving it to be supplied mentally by the reader or hearer, and usually it has to be supplied in the present tense (cf. 'me Tarzan, you Jane'). Some argue that where the surrounding verbs are in the past tense a past tense may also be supplied in these sentences. REB has taken this view and it allows us to understand that at some time in the past Amos had not been a *prophet* but *a herdsman and fig-grower*, prior to his call by God. Now it was on the strength of that call that he was entitled to *prophesy*. This may well be true but it is doubtful whether the point of the reply is to contrast what he once was with what he now was doing. More likely, Amos accepted Amaziah's assessment of him as a *seer* entitled to work in Judah and not a *prophet* entitled to work in Israel, but then went on to claim that it was YHWH who had given him the right, and the duty, to *prophesy against Israel*, and that was a higher authority than any official title could give him. A. G. Auld[7] goes further and thinks that Amos denied all claim to be a *prophet* and simply asserted that he must obey God and say what he was told to say. Only later, says Auld, was Amos called a prophet, and then by other people. Yet others have held that Amos was denying any 'professional' prophetic

[6] D. L. Petersen, *The Roles of Israel's Prophets* (*JSOT* Supplement 17), 1981, pp. 77–79.

[7] Auld, *Amos*, pp. 25–35.

role, since *prophet's son* refers to a member of a band or guild of prophets (cf. I Sam. 10.10); he was claiming to be a 'free lance'. There is something to be said for all these views but only one really comes to grips with the real question: where was Amos entitled to prophesy? Amaziah's answer was 'In Judah'; Amos' claim was 'In Israel'. But if 'in Israel' then by what authority? His reply makes a very clear contrast between the twice repeated emphatic *I* in v. 14 and the twice repeated *the* LORD in v. 15. Whatever Amos was or is was of little account; what did matter was the authority given to him by God's command to go and prophesy in Israel, although he was a Judaean. He could do no other than go (cf. 3.8).

Finally in v. 16 the pronoun is emphatic again. '*You tell me I am not to prophesy against Israel*', but since YHWH has told him to *prophesy to my people Israel* he proceeds with the words of the LORD in v.17. Neither Amaziah nor Jeroboam had authority to override the command of YHWH and to try to do so was to make themselves liable to his judgment. So Amaziah must share Israel's punishment; his *land* would *be parcelled out* and given away, he would *die in a heathen country*, his children would be killed and his wife be forced into prostitution to keep herself alive.

This question of authority, God's over against that of priests, kings and governments, has plagued not only Amos and Amaziah but people ever since. The book of Jeremiah with its account of his imprisonment for continuing to speak the words YHWH had given him is a further Old Testament example of it. It remained an issue in the New Testament for Jesus himself when the priests and scribes asked him, 'By what authority are you doing these things?', such as cleansing the Temple which was in the charge of the priests (Mark 11.29) or when he claimed to obey the Father, cost what it might, and demanded of his disciples that they do the same (John 15). Peter and John were faced with it when they were ordered to speak no more (Acts 3.18ff.). Church history is full of examples of those who knew that God's authority was supreme.

The fourth vision: Summer fruit

8.1–3 This important interruption over, the book returns to the description of the fourth vision. As we have said, Amos most probably saw with his own eyes *a basket of summer fruit*, presumably, though not certainly, in someone's hand. Where it was or where it was being taken we are not told and, though we may surmise that it was being taken to the sanctuary at Bethel for the celebration of the Feast of Tabernacles, that would be only a guess and indeed it doesn't matter. It was the Hebrew word translated *summer fruit* which caught his attention – *qayiṣ*, which reminded him of another word *qēṣ* meaning 'end'. This word-play or pun is perhaps the best known example in scripture (cf Jer. 1: 11, where *šākēd* means 'almond tree' and *šōkēd* 'on the watch'). The REB attempts to retain something of the word-play by using the word *ripe* as the footnote shows. So the threat is present again. The end had come for Israel. Israel was finished and once more there was no *pardon*. If there was some connection with the Feast of Tabernacles then we may compare this with 5. 18–20. Verse 3 may offer some support for this, for the first clause should probably read 'The temple-singers will howl'. This is better than *palace songs*. In any case the future held only the prospect of death with unburied *corpses* lying around. As in 5.13 and especially 6.10 no words were appropriate. There was nothing more to be said and to try might be dangerous. There is only *silence* left.

Whatever hopes Amos may have entertained in the first two visions, they had now been completely dashed and, however unwelcome this message was at Bethel, it had to be proclaimed because it was God's word.

Social behaviour and divine judgment

8.4–14 Although REB leaves no gap between vv. 3 and 4 and continues to print vv. 4–8 as prose, it is difficult to see how these verses can be a continuation of the vision report. It is better to think of a new section beginning at v. 4 criticizing social behaviour (vv. 4–8) and then threatening judgment (vv. 8–14) especially as it opens with '*Listen*' (cf 3.1; 4.1; 5.1).

8.4–8 Whether these verses can be rendered in the semi-poetical form of most of the rest of the book is uncertain. Many translations attempt this but REB has been content to leave it as prose. The dividing line between the two is not always very distinct. The content, though, is clear enough. In some ways the verses recall 2.6–7, but the emphasis is more on the merchants. It is they who *grind the poor* (cf. 2.7) and *suppress the humble*. The verb translated *suppress* is derived from the same root as *sabbath* and usually means 'to cause to cease' or 'bring to an end'. It is therefore a strong word. The thoughts of the merchants who do this are then quoted. *New moon*, a monthly occasion and *sabbath*, a weekly one, were days on which rest was enjoined. They often occur together (cf. Isa. 1.13) as special times instituted by God. In Ex. 20.8–11 the reason for keeping the sabbath was because God rested on the seventh day. In the form of the commandments recorded in Deut. 5, the reason was to remind people that God had delivered Israel from slavery in Egypt (vv. 12–16). According to Amos the merchants were so eager for profit that they could hardly wait for the rest days to come to an end, and the reasons for the days were far from their minds. Not only so, but they craved for the opportunity to give short measure and over-charge using doctored *scales* (cf. Deut. 25.13–16) and selling chaff among the *wheat*. Their wrongdoings have both a religious and a social aspect and the two things are not regarded as separate. In 2.6, as we saw, the subjects of the verbs were not specified and we surmised that the *they* probably referred to the wealthy landlords or landowners. Here in v. 6 a similar charge is laid against the merchants.

The response to these wrongs is another threat introduced by an oath as in 4.2 and 6.8. The oath is sworn *by the arrogance of Jacob* and this is curious because in 6.8 *the arrogance of Jacob* was what YHWH abhorred. How can he now swear by that which he abhors? We argued that in 6.8 it referred to that in which Jacob took pride, i.e. Samaria, but, if what was said about oaths in 4.2 is correct, YHWH should swear by something or someone at least as powerful as YHWH himself, such as *his holiness* or *himself*. Obviously Samaria cannot fulfil that role. We must probably conclude that the phrase means something different here. If we follow REB it would suggest that YHWH's oath is as secure and fixed as *the arrogance of Jacob*. We should expect, however, that as in the earlier two passages it refers to YHWH himself. It may be translated 'the pride of Jacob' and then it is possible to understand this to mean 'that in which Jacob ideally should take pride' i.e. YHWH. The content of the oath is awesome: *I shall never forget any of those activities of theirs*, especially when we recall that to remember or *never forget* a thing is not simply to retain the thing in the mind but is also to act upon it.

Verse 8 then fills out that threat by means of rhetorical questions expecting the answer 'yes'. There are some doubts, however, about the relation of this verse to what precedes and to what follows it. In the first place it seems to be a threat of disaster on a cosmic scale rather than an earthquake affecting only Israel. Secondly, something very similar occurs again in 9.5 as part of one of the hymnic passages (cf. 4.13; 5.8f.). It looks likely that either Amos himself or more probably his later interpreter added some lines from a hymn to round off vv. 4–7.

8.9–10   This is the first of three sayings referring to the coming *day* or *time*. Taken at face value v. 9 may refer to an eclipse of the sun and we are told that there had been one c. 763 BCE, probably a little before Amos' time. If an eclipse does underlie the passage it has almost certainly became a part of Amos' picture of the future when darkness would overcome light (cf. 5.18 and contrast John 1.5). Darkness and death are associated ideas and v.10 goes on to describe the mourning. Again there is an allusion to the *pilgrim-feasts*, probably the Feast of Tabernacles in particular, with its joyful celebration, instead of which there will be a day of bitter sorrow.

8.11–12   The second picture of the future depicts people frantically searching for food, not for literal food, but for the word of YHWH by which to live (Deut. 8.3). In the extremities of that future *time* people would look for the divine words which they have presently rejected, but it would be too late. God's final word had been spoken and it was one of destruction.

8.13–14   The third picture envisages that *young* people in the prime of life *will faint from thirst*, falling and dying. It may be connected with the previous verses, in which case the *thirst* like the *hunger* may be for the word of YHWH. More probably it is unrelated and simply describes the falling away of the most active and virile people (cf. Isa. 40.30, where only waiting on YHWH can renew strength). These are the ones who have worshipped foreign gods. The Hebrew speaks of the 'guilt' of *Samaria* but this hides the proper name *Ashimah*, a goddess who was certainly worshipped in Samaria c. 400 BCE, since she is mentioned in correspondence between Jews in Jerusalem and others in Elephantine in southern Egypt at that time. The god of *Dan* is not named. The *sacred way to Beersheba* probably hides another deity's name, for literally the Hebrew means 'As your way lives, Beersheba'. Just as 'guilt' hides the name of *Ashimah* so *sacred way* may hide a deity worshipped at Beersheba. However, if for the moment we omit the first line of v. 14 it is possible to understand the *god* of *Dan* as referring to YHWH and the *way to Beersheba* as also referring to him, especially as a similar word in Ugaritic to that translated 'way' means 'power'. The whole passage would then mean that fainting young people invoke YHWH from *Dan* to *Beersheba*, the extremities of David's Israel. But there will be no answer and they will perish. At some later stage the *god* of *Dan* and *way to Beersheba* were interpreted as references to other deities and so it was thought appropriate to add another, *Ashimah of Samaria*. This is an attractive way of understanding the passage since nowhere else does Amos have anything to say about Israel worshipping foreign gods. It allows us to retain all these pictures as Amos' words since there is nothing inconsistent with what Amos says elsewhere. Their meaning has been modified to suit new circumstances when his words were used to justify later threats against Judah.

The fifth vision: Strike the capitals

9.1–4   Chapter 9 opens with a fifth vision associated with Bethel like the previous four and in a similar but slightly different form (vv. 1–4). It is followed by the third hymn-like passage in the book (vv. 5–6) and further threats against Israel (vv. 7–8). But part way through v. 8 the whole tone changes and, as the new REB heading suggests, there follows a message of salvation and restoration (vv. 8–15) to conclude the book.

Although this vision threatens the destruction of the sanctuary and the inescapability of judgment for the people as do the visions of the *plumb-line* (or 'tin') and *summer fruit* it is probably wise to treat it separately. Obviously the editor of the book did not regard it as the fifth in a series or it would surely have followed on from the fourth. In this instance the vision is introduced by *I saw* rather than 'The Lord caused me to see or *showed me*'. There is none of the word-play found in the previous two and were it not for the introduction the vision itself would not be much different from many of the threats in the book. YHWH's presence at the sanctuary in Bethel was not in doubt. He was *standing by the altar*. What would be surprising would be Amos' claim that the word YHWH spoke was one of threat against the sanctuary and its worshippers. The message is clear enough, the only point of uncertainty being the question of who is commanded by God to *strike the capitals*. Some commentators have suggested changing the text to bring it more into line with the earlier visions 'striking the capitals. . . .', and transferring *and he said* to follow *is shaken*. The Hebrew, however, is perfectly grammatical as it stands and should be retained as in REB. The command to '*strike*. . . .' must be understood in one of two ways. First, it may be addressed to one of YHWH's heavenly messengers, a member of the divine king's court. Evidence that YHWH was envisaged as King surrounded, like any king, by a circle of courtiers, superhuman beings, may be found in Job 1. 10ff. and Isa. 6, while heavenly messengers feature also in the patriarchal stories (cf. Gen. 18). Second, it may be addressed to the prophet himself since, as we have seen (cf. on 1. 3–6), by speaking the word of God the prophet played a part in the fulfilment of that word. The threat itself recalls the exploit of Samson at Gaza (Judg. 16.18ff.) though whether this was intentional or coincidental we cannot say. The people crushed under the weight of the Temple would, of course, have been those at worship there and, since Bethel was the royal shrine, they may have been largely the people at court. Verses 2–3, which warned that there was no escape, echo the words of Ps. 139.7–12. Again we cannot be sure that this was intentional. In any case their meaning was reversed. In the psalm YHWH's presence wherever people may go is welcomed as it assures them of his blessing. Here his presence is for the purpose of judgment and it is just as inescapable. The *serpent* which *will bite them* (cf. 5.19) in v. 3 is well known in certain Ancient Near Eastern creation myths. It was imprisoned in the sea by the god of creation. The roaring of the sea could then be thought of as the serpent or dragon struggling to get free (Job 3.8; 7.12; Ps. 74.12–14; Isa. 27.1). This does not mean that Amos believed the myth. The biblical writers were not afraid to use mythological language and pictures to clothe their message. That

YHWH will *fix* his *eye on them for evil* (v. 4) is again a reversal of what would be expected. Instead of watching over them to protect them he would watch to punish them (cf. Job 7.19–21). So divine judgment was inevitable and inescapable.

Yahweh, Israel and the nations

9.5–8*a*

9.5–6   This is the third hymn-like passage, similar to 4.13 and 5.8–9 and also to 8.8. It has the same function as the others: to underscore the judgment which has been pronounced. The emphasis is not so much on the act of creation but more on YHWH's control of all nature. The statement that *the earth heaves* and *surges like the Nile* may suggest an earthquake, and *summons the waters of the sea and pours them over the earth* suggests a subsequent flood, but we should not think of some historical incident. The language is that of the hymn of praise. This, though, is the God with whom Israel has to deal.

Verses 7–8*a*   In this remarkable passage Amos denied to Israel the special relationship with YHWH of which the people were so proud and which gave them ground, mistakenly, for self-confidence. It was undeniable that YHWH brought *Israel up from Egypt*, but the implications of that for their status before YHWH were no different from those arising from the fact that he brought *the Philistines from Caphtor* (Crete) and *the Aramaeans* (Syrians) *from Kir*. Israel was now on a par with them, no different from *the Cushites* (Ethiopians). So towards the end of the book Amos is depicted as returning to the claims that he had made at the beginning (1.3–2.16). We should beware of reading too much into this. Amos was not setting out his theological position with regard to the relationship between YHWH and his people and the rest of the world. His purpose was to affirm that Israel had forfeited its special status and was to be judged like any other nation. Again, the eyes of YHWH were *on* the *sinful kingdom*, and he would *destroy it from the face of the earth*.

A remnant spared and restored
Amos 9.8b–15

9.8b After all the uncompromising threats of darkness and disaster in the book of Amos and even in the preceding lines of this verse this line comes as a surprise and leaves an uncomfortable feeling that someone at a later date and for some reason has wished to modify Amos' message. To that extent REB is right to regard it as the beginning of a new section. But *yet*, or 'except that', firmly links it with what has gone before and *says the LORD* rounds off the saying. The line, therefore, is a connecting line between the preceding threats and the message of hope which is to follow.

9.9–10 The first two verses of this message of hope are not easy to understand. By translating 8b as *I shall not totally destroy Jacob's posterity* and linking it to v. 9 with *No*, by seeing vv. 9–10 as a metaphor of *a sieve* and by the translation *all the sinners of my people* in v. 10, REB seems to have taken these verses to mean that some Israelites, presumably the good ones, will be spared. Whether the *pebble* represents good Israelites who will be preserved or the bad Israelites who will later be thrown away while the good pass through the *sieve* to safety is hard to say and it doesn't affect the meaning. However, the fact that Israel was placed in the *sieve among all the nations* suggests rather a sifting process to separate Israel from the nations rather than the good Israelites from the bad. Moreover, such distinction between the fate of good and bad seems foreign to the pre-exilic and exilic prophets, where it is usually the whole nation which would be punished. Of course, when Amos spoke of the end of Israel he was not thinking that every single Israelite would be killed. He was simply using forceful language; but nowhere does he or any later prophet suggest that all the wicked will be destroyed and the good spared. So we should not think that this is the meaning of the present passage, whether it comes from Amos himself or from his later followers. In fact, v. 8b does not suggest such a separation; it simply states that destruction will not be total. In v. 10 it is by no means sure that the Hebrew behind *all the sinners of my people* intends such a distinction. That would probably require a different construction. The phrase may mean no more than 'my people who are all sinners'.

Besides all this the metaphor of a *sieve* is not found elsewhere and the Hebrew word used here means *sieve* nowhere else. In I Sam. 19.13, 16 a word from the same root is translated 'rug'; another in II Kings 8.15 as 'blanket' and another in Ex. 27.4; 35.16 as 'grating'. What these have in common is woven threads of fibre or metal and that is how the translation *sieve* is reached. Further, the word *pebble* is found only here and in II Sam. 17.13, where it is translated 'stone' in the context of destroying a town and leaving no stone upon another. The word *shake* normally means 'to stagger' or 'to totter' and has been used twice by Amos in 4.8 and 8.12, where REB translated *stagger* (evidently in the sense of wandering aimlessly). Moreover the Hebrew does not speak of the sieve being shaken; it speaks of something or someone – the verb is used impersonally – being shaken in a sieve, assuming those are the correct meanings. The Septuagint doesn't speak of a shaking or of a sieve but of 'winnowing' with a 'winnowing fan' and 'something smashed' falling to the ground. Obviously it interpreted the metaphor differently while still keeping the notion of separation.

To return to the beginning of the verse, we should translate 'See! I am about to issue a command' but it does not say to whom the command is given and what is more, what follows is not a command, nor is there a command in sight.

All these considerations will show how hard it is to be sure of the meaning of the verse. Tentatively I should like to suggest that the uncertainty is caused by the transformation of an original Amos oracle of destruction into a later Judaean message of hope. We may reconstruct the original as follows:

> For see! I am going to cause distress
> I will cause the house of Israel to wander among all the nations
> (Like whoever wanders in the distance)
> The bag he carries will never rest on the ground
> By the sword my people who are all sinners will die.

This translation (and interpretation) is so different from the usual that it demands a fuller explanation.

First, it assumes that a common word 'going to issue a command' has been accidentally misread or miscopied for a similar but rare word meaning 'going to cause distress'. Second, the word translated *shake* has been translated in the same way as in 4.8 and 8.12 as mentioned above. Third, the line in parenthesis takes the Hebrew word translated *sieve* by REB as meaning 'in the distance'. There is perhaps some little support for this rendering in the fact that the verb 'to wander' is the same as is used of Cain, who was condemned to be a wanderer and fugitive on the earth (cf. Hos. 9.17). It is placed in brackets because, if translated in the more usual way, it may have been added later by way of explanation. Fourth, the translation 'bag' instead of *pebble* is based on the rendering in Gen. 42.35 and Prov. 7.20 etc. The passage is then a threat of deportation and destruction.

When the oracle came to be used later in Judah, where a more hopeful future was eventually expected, the similarity of the language with that of the sieve metaphor made it readily available and adaptable. Possibly, even the line about the *sieve* being *shaken to and fro* may have been added at this time to explain the adaptation, if the translation above in brackets is thought to be too far-fetched.

9.11–12   It was therefore natural to continue with an oracle about the restoration of *David's fallen house*. The Hebrew, in fact, speaks of David's fallen booth, the same word as is used in the name of the Feast of Tabernacles or Booths. This is the only occurrence of the phrase and so there are no other passages to help us. It may refer to the Davidic dynasty and look forward to a new Davidic line (cf. Isa. 11.1–9), but the second half of v. 11 implies a building and it is better to think of either the Temple or, more probably, Jerusalem. In Isa. 4.5, a later passage looking to the future, Jerusalem will have a 'booth' to shield it from all damage. This would mean that when these verses were spoken or written Jerusalem was in ruins, that is, after 587 BCE. During the exile, as we have seen (cf. on 1.11–12) *Edom* encroached on Judah's territory, and the promise here is that post-exilic *Israel*, not the Northern Kingdom, will repossess the territory and gain ascendancy over *all the nations* which had once been ruled by David.

9.13–15   The previous verses have looked backwards to the time of David and forwards to a comparable era in the future with a new, rebuilt Jerusalem. That age, just like the new Davidic age in Isa. 11.1–9, would be one of peace and prosperity when harvest would follow immediately on the sowing of seed! Again, the great harvest Feast of Tabernacles was probably in mind when there would be a superabundance of grapes with the juice running like rivers on the hills. Each year at the Feast God restored *the fortunes of Israel* by sending the rains. Even more remarkable would it be on this future day. This was the original meaning of the phrase *restore the fortunes* but it came to refer specifically to the return from exile – hence the traditional but mistaken translation 'turn again the captivity of . . .'. So v. 14 recalls the threat of Amos himself in 5.11 but reverses it, while v. 15 sees Israel permanently resettled in its God-given land.

The promise that they would *never again be uprooted* has not, of course, been fulfilled, for the Jews certainly have been *uprooted* from their own *soil* and only this century have been allowed to return there. The belief expressed here remains part of the equation in any solution of modern Jewish-Arab relationships.

It is worth noticing that these hopes for the future expressed at the conclusion of the book are not made dependent on the repentance of Israel. The restoration comes from YHWH alone as a result of his enduring love and grace. This is true also for other writings which anticipate the return from exile like Ezekiel and Isaiah 40–55, where the honour of God's name or reputation, rather than a change of heart among his people, lies behind YHWH's redeeming activity. Just as the first exodus from Egypt must be attributed to the prior love of God (Deut. 7.6ff.) so the second exodus, the return from exile in Babylon and restoration to the promised land, is also an act of sheer grace. The imagery is carried over into the New Testament, for it is the same love and grace which, Christians believe, prompted the sending of Jesus to restore not only Israel to the promised land, but all mankind to that relationship with God in which all people may find their fulfilment and joy.

The message of Amos is one of unrelieved gloom and pessimism for eighth-century BCE Israel. This is balanced in the final form of the book by a hope for the future of the people of God, both Judah and Israel. As has been said earlier, we need to take very seriously both these messages, heeding the threats of Amos and giving thanks for the hopes of his interpreters and remembering that both threat and hope have their place in the Christian gospel.

HOSEA

Introduction

The book of Hosea brings into sharper focus than the book of Amos the need to distinguish between the words spoken by the prophet and the message of the book as we now have it.[1] If we read the book in its present form, as we are entitled to do, it is clear that if foretells as terrible a judgment on Israel as Amos does but then also offers hope for the nation. Yet as we shall see it is quite possible, even probable, that Hosea in his preaching held out no such hope. The question to be faced by the interpreter is whether to interpret what the prophet may be thought to have said to the Israel of his day and leave the rest on one side or to expound the message of the book as it now presents itself to us having come from the hands of preachers and editors who were keen to show the relevance of Hosea's teaching for their own day. This commentary seeks to avoid that choice because the writer believes that both messages are valid and both need to be expounded for the benefit of today's readers and preachers.

Ideally it would be best to begin with the teaching of Hosea as it is presented to us in chs. 4–14 before considering the accounts of his marriage and the birth of his children in chs. 1–3. It would be safer to interpret the latter in the light of the former rather than the former in the light of the latter, especially since the problems surrounding chs. 1–3 are many and have long been recognized. To do this, however, would make the commentary more difficult to use and therefore the idea has been rejected, though the reader may, if he wishes, leave chs. 1–3 until the end. The fact of the matter is that if we possessed only chs. 4–14 we should probably answer the question about hope in Hosea's teaching very differently, for there are only two passages which seem to offer it to Israel. As in the book of Amos, the final chapter does so and that may be interpreted in much the

---

[1] For a full discussion of this matter, cf. G.I. Emmerson, *Hosea: an Israelite Prophet in Judaean Perspective*, although the author comes to different conclusions from the views set out in this commentary.

same way as the closing verses of Amos. The other place where hope is offered is in the well-known ch. 11. That being so, we should want to look very closely at that chapter to see how it may be reconciled with the harsh judgmental tone of the rest of the book. It is largely because we are influenced by what we read in chs. 1–3 that we are ready to accept, almost without question, the message of hope in ch. 11 as coming from Hosea himself in spite of its incongruence with the remainder of Hosea's teaching.

Chapters 1–3, as we shall see, are full of difficulties themselves. Certainly they tell us all we can know about Hosea apart from any hints which may be found in the rest of the book as a result of the kind of metaphors and language he uses, and evidence such as this is very unreliable. At first sight they seem to tell us a great deal about Hosea's personal affairs, much more, in fact, than we know about any other prophet except perhaps Jeremiah, and there are now big question-marks over the biographical material in that book as well. By piecing together chs. 1 and 3 we ought to be able to obtain a clear picture of Hosea's family life, but as soon as we make the attempt we run into difficulties. Ch. 1 is written about Hosea by someone else; ch. 3 ostensibly comes from Hosea himself. Our instinct, therefore, would be to begin with ch. 3 as the more likely to be reliable, but we shall see that not all accounts written in the first person are really autobiographical. Though both accounts tell of a marriage, ch. 1 seems to be more interested in the birth of his children and their names. When scholars have compared the accounts of his marriage in the two chapters they have come to very different conclusions, for it is not clear whether they both speak of the same event or whether ch. 3 speaks of a reconciliation following an unmentioned separation or whether ch. 3 tells of a second marriage to a different woman. The answer to these questions will determine the interpretation of God's dealings with Israel and we shall have to consider them more fully in the commentary itself. Enough to say that the answer we give will have some bearing on the question mentioned earlier as to whether Hosea himself offered any hope to Israel.

There is one other factor which has a bearing on this dilemma about Hosea's teaching. If he did proclaim a hope for the Israel of his day, he was surely wrong and Amos was right, for Israel was finally overcome and overrun by the Assyrians in 722 BCE. In 735 Israel and Syria had entered into a coalition to withstand Assyrian pressure westwards and had sought to coerce Judah into joining with them.

While Isaiah refers to this from a Judaean point of view (Isa. 7) Hosea does so from the Israelite standpoint (5.8–6.6). The Syro-Ephraimite alliance, as it is usually called, proved to be ineffective. The Assyrians captured Damascus in 732 BCE. At the same time they annexed a large part of Israel's territory, leaving Samaria and the surrounding area intact but placing the pro-Assyrian Hoshea on the throne of the reduced state. In 727 he decided to rebel and the Assyrians attacked again. They took Samaria in 722 after a long siege and dispersed large numbers of inhabitants in different parts of the Assyrian empire (II Kings 17.20ff.). Their place was taken by foreigners brought in from elsewhere. So Israel virtually disappeared from view until its people emerged again in the fifth century BCE as the Samaritans. It is possible, of course, that Hosea simply got it wrong, though why anyone should want to preserve the prophecies of a prophet who was so dramatically wrong is hard to understand, especially since the Deuteronomists, who are thought probably to have gathered the prophetic material together, had argued that a prophet was to be judged true or false according to whether his prophecies were fulfilled or not (Deut. 18.21f.) It is possible, and it is permissible for us in our day, to argue that the hopes expressed here were ultimately fulfilled in Jesus Christ in a way more profound than Hosea could have imagined, but that would have made no sense to his hearers or to his successors who preserved these accounts and prophecies.

We can see, however, that in Judah, the Southern Kingdom, in the following centuries there were hopes of a united kingdom associated with a new coming David (Jer. 31.31; Ezek. 37.15ff.). We are bound to consider the strong possibility that Hosea's words of judgment, like Amos', were carried south to Judah in or after 722 BCE to be used again in condemnation of Judah and as a warning to its people and its leaders. Once more, like Amos' words, Hosea's teaching would be reinterpreted in the light of Judaean hopes that were current, and these reinterpretations could then become incorporated as part of the final book.

We must therefore beware of beginning our study with the often stated assumption that Hosea was somehow gentler than Amos because he was a native Israelite and that therefore he could offer hope as against Amos' total condemnation. After all, both were convinced that they were passing on the word of God and not their own. Hosea would surely have recoiled from the idea that he was watering down his message on account of his identification with the people under threat.

One further point about the book of Hosea needs to be mentioned, and that concerns the Hebrew text. A glance at the number of footnotes in the English versions, especially in RSV, will show that the difficulties of being sure about the meaning are greater than in almost any other book in the Old Testament. Often translators have to make use of the Greek and Syriac versions and have to suggest changes to the Hebrew text in order to make sense of it. The reason for this problem is not clear. It may be that the text became damaged or miscopied in the course of transmission, especially as it passed from Israel into Judah. Another possibility is that Hosea spoke a Northern dialect and since he is the only Northern (Israelite) prophet whose words have been preserved we are unfamiliar with some of his terms. Whatever the reason, the fact remains that at many points we have to make difficult decisions about meaning. This will explain wide differences in the English translations and the tentative nature of some of the interpretations offered in this and in other commentaries.

Commentary

Introductory Verse

1.1 The book of Hosea, like the book of Amos, opens with an introductory verse provided by the final editor in which the names of the Judaean kings precede those of the Israelite kings. This reflects the Judaean perspective from which the final form of the book was composed. No less than four Judaean kings are mentioned, suggesting that Hosea was active before the death of Uzziah in c. 745 BCE and continued to be so until the reign of Hezekiah which began c. 715 BCE. His would therefore be a long ministry. However since Samaria, the capital of Israel, fell in 722 BCE and the Northern Kingdom then became part of an Assyrian province, it is doubtful whether Hosea was still active in 715. Certainly there is nothing in the book to suggest that this is so, and from its perspective the events of 722 are still future. From the material in the book we may say that Hosea was active from c. 745 certainly to sometime beyond the Syro-Ephraimite alliance in 735 BCE. The mention of Hezekiah's name in this opening verse suggests that Hosea's words to the Northern Kingdom were preserved and carried into Judah after 722, where they continued to be used and reinterpreted in whatever way was necessary as a threat to Judah when that nation too was threatened by Assyria at the very end of the eighth century BCE. It is probable that they were recalled and re-used even later than that until Judah itself was taken into captivity in Babylon in 587 BCE.

While the Judaean kings mentioned by the editor suggest too long a period of Hosea's ministry the Northern king mentioned suggests too short a period, for only Jeroboam II is mentioned and he died c. 752 BCE. The absolute dates of the kings of Israel and Judah are uncertain and different scholars assign different dates to them. This is not of major significance, however, for our purpose. What is important is that there are sayings in the book of Hosea which come from a period after Jeroboam's death. As we have already noted, there are passages which deal with the Syro-Ephraimite alliance in 735 BCE and others which fit well into the period after the fall of Damascus in 732 BCE and the annexation by the Assyrians of a considerable part of Israel's territory. During the time between Jeroboam's death and the fall of Damascus Israel had many kings. Jeroboam's son, Zechariah, succeeded him but was assassinated after six months by Shallum, who became king though he was not a member of the dynasty of Jehu. A month or so later he in turn was killed by Menahem, a usurper, who reigned c. 750–741 and followed a pro-Assyrian policy (II Kings 15.19). Then he was succeeded by Pekahiah, who reigned for two years before being ousted by Pekah (c. 740–730), who was involved in the Syro-Ephraimite alliance. When the Assyrians annexed much of Israelite territory, Hoshea became king with Assyrian support and ruled over what was left, namely Samaria and the surrounding territory. He later rebelled and sought Egyptian help (II Kings 17.4). The Assyrians besieged Samaria and after lengthy resistance it fell in 722 BCE. We are entitled to ask why the editor of Hosea fails to mention all this in his introduction, but we can find no answer. It may have been that he found the list too long and confusing to include or that he regarded it as of no importance or that he regarded these kings as wholly illegitimate rulers, even more so than Jeroboam. It is possible, as we shall see, that Hosea himself referred to this quick succession of kings (e.g. in 8.4) though other interpretations are also possible. However, we must see this unsettled period as the background to much that Hosea had to say to Israel.

Of Hosea's personal background we are told only the name of his father. Since Hosea's children, a little later in this chapter, were given symbolic and meaningful names we may ask whether the same is true of him and his father. *Hosea* is derived from the verb 'to save' as are Joshua and Isaiah. There was also a contemporary king Hoshea. It would seem therefore that this type of name was common enough and there is no need to read any symbolic meaning into it. His father was called *Beeri*. If we translate that it means 'my well' and again we can discover no hidden significance in it. The only other person in the Old Testament with this name was Esau's father-in-law! It is best simply to regard this as a customary way of introducing a person by reference to his parentage.

Hosea's marriage
Hosea 1.2–3.5

'Go, take an unchaste woman'

1.2–9 This is said to be *the beginning of the* Lord*'s message given by Hosea* but, in fact, what follows is an account by someone else, not Hosea, of his marriage and the birth of his three children. The opening words mean that the editor who put them there saw these events as part of Hosea's message to Israel. Their intention, therefore, is not to give us information about Hosea but to tell us what God was saying to Israel. Nor was the marriage simply the result of mutual attraction or parental arrangement. It was commanded by God, *Go and take an unchaste woman as your wife.* Now it is important to take this command very seriously. There have been, and still are, those who find it difficult to believe that God would command his prophet to do such a thing.[1] They look for an interpretation of this command other than the straightforward one. Some have argued that the description of *Gomer* as *an unchaste woman* is a result of hindsight, that she was chaste when Hosea married her but became unfaithful later. Looking back and recounting the marriage, she could therefore be described as *unchaste* from the point of view of the writer. Such a view may be thought to gain some support from the fact that the marriage is meant in some way to represent the relationship between YHWH and Israel. Since Israel was 'chaste' when God chose her and became *unchaste* later the same must be true of Hosea and Gomer. On this view it has been argued that Hosea learned the extent and nature of YHWH's love for unfaithful Israel through his personal

[1] For a full discussion and bibliography up to 1956 see H.H. Rowley, 'The Marriage of Hosea', *BJRL* 39, 1956–57, pp. 200–33, reprinted in *Men of God*, Nelson 1963, pp. 66–97.

experience of loving a woman who became unfaithful. This, however, is not what the text says. Verse 2 states clearly that Hosea was told to *go and take an unchaste woman*. The relationship between YHWH and Israel in the past is of no immediate concern. Israel is now unfaithful and to proclaim that unfaithfulness Hosea was to marry *an unchaste woman*. It is, of course, an extraordinary thing but prophets were, from time to time, told to do extraordinary things. Isaiah was to walk naked and barefoot through Jerusalem to proclaim the coming captivity of Judah (ch. 20). Jeremiah was forbidden to marry at all (16.1), and then had to walk in Jerusalem wearing a wooden yoke as an expression of YHWH's will that Judah must submit to the Babylonians (chs. 27–28). In Ezek. 24.15ff. we read that the prophet was to forego all mourning rites when his wife died, the dearest thing he had, as a means of proclaiming the greater disaster of the fall of Jerusalem. Hosea's marriage was an action of the same kind. It was *the LORD's message* proclaimed in the most startling way.

Others have regarded the whole chapter as allegorical and not a description of a real marriage at all. Against this view is the fact that if it were an allegory, all the names involved ought to have some symbolic meaning and not just those of the three children. But *Gomer*, if it means anything at all, seems to be derived from a Hebrew root meaning 'to come to an end', of which it would probably be a masculine participle. Such a meaning of the name of Hosea's wife makes little sense. Her father's name *Diblaim* appears to mean 'a couple of figs' and although it has been suggested that it means his daughter could be had for a couple of figs this seems far-fetched. There seems to be no reason, therefore, to take this verse other than at face value. There remains the question as to what exactly is meant by *an unchaste woman*. As we shall discover later on, Hosea had a good deal to say about the sexual activities associated with Canaanite rites performed in the worship of Baal and about Israel's participation in these. It may be, therefore, that Gomer was a cultic prostitute involved in these activities. Others have argued that the first intercourse of all Israelite girls took place as a part of these rites. All these are to some extent speculation. In whatever way her unchastity had come about, Hosea's marriage to her would come as a surprising and shocking thing, and every time Hosea walked out with his *unchaste woman* it would be a condemnation of Israel's unfaithfulness to YHWH, *for like an unchaste woman this land is guilty of unfaithfulness to the LORD.*

The marriage sign is then quickly left behind and attention is directed to the children of the marriage, who are the main concern of the passage. Perhaps too much attention is paid to the marriage itself, which serves only to introduce the children and explain the background to their symbolic names, which themselves point to a gradual deterioration in the relationship between YHWH and Israel. Isaiah too gave his children symbolic names and was told to go out with one of them to meet the king. The name of the child would give a message to the king (Isa. 7.1ff.). So here the people, seeing the children around and knowing their names, would be reminded of *the LORD's message*. Hosea's children were a boy, a girl and another boy. Again there seems to be no symbolism behind this alternation of the sexes and we should therefore accept that this is what happened. Strictly speaking, only the first child is explicitly said to be his. Gomer *bore him a son* in v. 3 but *bore a daughter* in v. 6 and *bore a son* in v. 8. Some people have thought the last two were not Hosea's children but were the result of Gomer's infidelity. This is probably to press the detail of the account too far and make too much of the omission of *him* in vv. 6 and 8.

The first son was to be called *Jezreel*. Perhaps to Israelites who knew Hosea and his family the name would be ambiguous. *Jezreel* was the valley which ran from Mount Carmel in a south-easterly direction to the Jordan. It divided the Galilean area from the central or southern area of Israel. It was a fertile valley and became the very symbol of fertility and prosperity. Although the capital of Israel was in Samaria, the kings of Israel seem to have had a summer palace in Jezreel. Ahab went there to avoid the storm following the contest on Mount Carmel between Elijah and the prophets of Baal (I Kings 18.46) and Naboth had a vineyard there adjoining Ahab's palace (I Kings 21.1). It was there that Jehu carried out a bloody purge of all the family of Ahab when he organized a coup against the Omride dynasty and established a new dynasty of which Jeroboam II was the current monarch (II Kings 9.14ff.). It is to this negative connotation of *Jezreel* that the present text draws attention, for the name is interpreted as a threat to the dynasty of Jehu on account of the purge. This is somewhat surprising because Jehu's coup was instigated by YHWH through Elijah (I Kings 19.16) and Elisha (II Kings 9.1ff.) as was the purge of the royal family. Now, said Hosea, the present member of Jehu's family would be punished for the purge Jehu carried out at God's command, according to the writer of Kings. We must assume either that the purge was even more ruthless than YHWH intended, which is hardly likely since the order to Elijah was total destruction, or that Hosea knew nothing of the tradition now found in I and II Kings regarding Elijah's and Elisha's part in the coup. In any case, as a result of it the *the kingdom of Israel* or possibly 'kingship in Israel' will come *to an end*. Israel as an independent kingdom with its own monarchy will be no more. Later on in the book we shall come across other passages where it is difficult to say whether Hosea was opposed to the contemporary kings, or to the Northern 'schismatic' monarchy which had broken away from the Davidic dynasty in Judah or to monarchy as an institution. In the present context the question is less important. Israel and its monarchy were so tied up together that if one came to an end, so did the other. *Israel's bow* refers to its military strength (cf. I Sam. 2.4 where 'strong men' is literally 'the bow of the warriors', and Jer. 49.35) focussed in the royal court at *Jezreel*. The place of prosperity and the place of the apparently sinful coup will become the place of defeat and destruction.

The second child (v. 6) is given a name of unusual form. *Ruhamah* is a feminine participle passive from a verb meaning 'to take pity on' preceded by the negative particle *Lo*. It therefore means 'she is not pitied' or 'she is not the object of compassion'. This is rather better that REB's 'not loved' in the footnote and *show love* in the text. The word 'pity' or 'compassion' often contains a hint of forgiveness or at least a cessation of anger (cf. Deut. 13.17; 30.3). So the threat of *Jezreel* will be carried out without compassion. God will not relent.

1.7 is an excellent example of the way in which an oracle against Israel was used again in Judah.[2] The compiler who told the story of Hosea's marriage and the birth of his children was doing so in the context of events in the Southern Kingdom of Judah. He therefore saw Hosea's second child as an unrelenting threat against Israel. Doubtless he was aware of Judah's similar failings, but always in Judah the severe threats were accompanied by hope for the future. He therefore added this verse, almost as a parenthesis, to assure his Judaean hearers or readers that YHWH would have compassion on Judah and would save that nation. His insistence that YHWH alone would do this without armaments reminds us of Isaiah's similar insistence on reliance on YHWH and not on the strength of arms

---

[2] But cf. Emmerson. *Hosea*, pp. 88 ff.

during the crisis of 701 BCE when Judah was under attack from the Assyrians (Isa. 31.1–3). Both are drawing on an ancient tradition, sometimes called the 'Holy War' or the 'Yahweh war' tradition. It may be seen at the Red Sea (Ex. 14.14), the capture of Jericho (Josh. 7), the victory of Gideon (Judg. 7, and cf. the note on Amos 5.18). No pity, then, for Israel but pity for Judah. Both messages need to be taken to heart, for both are part of the teaching of the book of Hosea (see Introduction, p.97.).

The third child had a name made up of a noun, again preceded by a negative. *Lo-ammi* means *not my people* and it denotes the final severance of the special relationship between YHWH and Israel brought into being in the time of Moses at the exodus from Egypt. There YHWH chose this group of people to be 'his people'. The phrase 'you shall be my people and I shall be your God' is sometimes called the 'covenant formula', giving definition to the relationship (Jer. 31.33; 32.38). It is uncertain, however, at what stage in its history Israel understood its relation to God in terms of a covenant. The majority of references to 'covenant' are later than Deuteronomy, though some seem to be earlier. In all probability 'covenant' was used alongside other relational terms, but the Deuteronomists made it the dominant means of defining the relationship. In any case 'my people' is used by YHWH of Israel prior to the account of the 'covenant' ceremony at Sinai in Exodus 24. The story in Exodus 3 has YHWH call them 'my people' as he spoke to Moses at the burning bush (Ex. 3.7). This is now negated by the name of Hosea's third child. Israel has forfeited the right to use the term and has put itself back to the status it had before Moses. As the REB footnote indicates, the second line of this couplet reads in Hebrew *and I shall not be* 'to or for you'. This again takes us back to Exodus 3 and the burning bush, for it was there that YHWH revealed his name and its meaning to Moses. The very name YHWH is connected with the verb 'to be' in the sense of 'to be with' and not simply 'to exist'. So, even before the name was given, YHWH promised 'I am with you' (Ex. 3.12), and there begins the story of YHWH's being 'with' and 'for' Israel. That part of the promise is also abrogated in this third child of Hosea. No longer is YHWH for Israel. They are on their own and the relationship begun at the exodus is now completely annulled.

So the three children coming at roughly two-year intervals, were signs that the special relationship between YHWH and Israel had been gradually deteriorating and was now finally broken. So far, therefore, the message is the same as that given through Amos and, whatever we may decide about certain more hopeful passages later, nothing should obscure the fact that if a people does persistently show itself unfaithful to God then God may in the end turn away and leave it to its own fate (cf. 5.6).

Reunion and a new hope

1.10–2.1   In the Hebrew Bible v. 9 brings us to the end of the first chapter; vv. 10 and 11 are the opening verses of ch. 2. The significance of this is that the connection between vv. 2–9 and 10–11 was much less close than REB and other English versions suggest, so far as those Jews were concerned who divided the Hebrew text into chapters and verses. Moreover v. 10 is the exact reverse of v. 9 with nothing at all between to explain the reversal of the threat. It can only have come from a very different situation. The clue to that is in v. 11, which says that *Judah and Israel will be reunited and will choose for themselves one leader.* As was pointed out in the Introduction (p. 97), this idea became current in the days of Jeremiah and Ezekiel, perhaps fostered by King Josiah's attempts to bring Samaria back under Judaean control (II Kings 23.15ff.) In Jer. 31.31 the new covenant will be with 'the people of Israel and Judah.' In Ezek. 37.15f. the prophet was to take two wooden tablets. On one he was to write Judah . . . and on the other Israel . . . and then 'bring the two together to form one tablet'. 'No longer will they be two nations' (v. 22); 'I shall be their God and they will be my people' (v. 27), and 'my servant David will be king over them' (v. 24). As with v. 7 so in vv. 10–11 we have a further illustration of the way a prophet's threats could be used again probably within a century or so of their being made by the prophet; but, applied to the new situation in Judah c. 600 BCE, they needed to be supplemented by the promise. Both threat and promise need to be heard again in the light of each new set of circumstances.

'Call your mother to account'

2.2–17   This long poem describes the relationship between YHWH and Israel in terms of a court case involving an unfaithful wife and mother. It is often difficult to tell which is in the forefront of the speaker or writer's mind, Israel or the wife, for reality and metaphor are very closely intertwined. *Call your mother to account* is almost equivalent to 'take your mother to court'. This address to the children links it with ch. 1. It is as though the severance of the relationship, *she is no longer my wife nor am I her husband*, makes it inappropriate for the husband himself to bring a charge against his wife; but the children are still her children and she their mother and so they are entitled to press the case. In fact, though, as the poem unfolds the chidren play little part in the conduct of the case. It is YHWH the husband who accuses Israel and acts as judge at the same time. Probably we should not press the legal analogy too far. Any unfaithful wife was, of course, guilty at law and the sentence would be death by stoning (Ex. 20.14; Deut. 5.18; Lev. 18.20; 20.10 and cf. John 8.1–11), whether she were tried before some central court or by the local elders at the town gate (cf. Amos 5.10). Initially in v. 2 there is an opportunity for her (i.e. Israel) to *put an end to her infidelity*. The threat that he will *parade her naked* as punishment leads to the thought of Israel in *the wilderness* where the people were led by YHWH. Now, however, she will be left to die of thirst. The statement in v. 4 that YHWH will *show no love towards her children* can scarcely mean the three children Gomer had by Hosea. More probably it refers to the Israelite descendants. Certainly v. 5 is a clear reference to Israel's settlement in Canaan and its readiness to seek help from Canaanite baals (local manifestations of the high god Baal) instead of from YHWH. In the wilderness the people had learned to rely on YHWH but in Canaan, where Baal was thought to be in control of rain and fertility, they had fallen into the trap of thinking that YHWH might not be adequate to the task. They had therefore worshipped Baal as well as, if not instead of YHWH. New cultural and intellectual climates always present a challenge to traditional religious belief.

The phrase *that is why* in vv. 6, 9 and 14 (where REB translates the same word as *But now*) divides the poem into four sections. Verses 6–8 seem to move towards a reconciliation. YHWH will seek to prevent Israel from recognizing and seeking help from the baals, *her lovers*. As a result of his activity they will come to realize that they

107

were better off with YHWH. Because of its different tone some have regarded this as a later section which has been included at this point. There is no need to question it, however, for although it offers the possibility of change it ends in v. 8 with the assertion that Israel *does not know that it was I who gave her.* . . . and what YHWH had given they offered to Baal in gratitude. The section ends where the previous one ended, with Israel guilty.

The third section makes very clear that any attempts at reconciliation have proved abortive. It threatens that YHWH will take away all the good things he has given Israel. The verdict in the case is clear and the punishment again is nakedness with *no one to rescue her.* The *merrymaking* associated with the festivals and the *festivals* themselves will come to and end (cf. Amos 5.21–23). Whereas for Amos the fault in Israel's worship was that they forgot YHWH and ignored his will in everyday life, for Hosea worship is to be brought to an end because the *holy days* and *sacrifices* are offered *to the baalim*. In the few years between the two prophets there seems to have been an increase in the practices associated with Baal worship. The very unsettled period at the end of the reign of Jeroboam II and during the following years when king followed king in quick succession (see note on 1.1) seems to have brought with it a resurgence of Baalism which threatened the continuance of the nation. This third section ends with the concluding formula *This is the word of the LORD* (v. 13).

It is not, however, the end of the poem as we have it, for there is a fourth section (vv. 14–19) which like the second and third begins with 'that is why'. REB has translated it differently (*but now*) because 'that is why' would suggest that a reason has been given in the previous verses for what is now to follow, whereas no grounds are stated for the message of restoration which comes next. The passage speaks as though Israel were in Egypt again and about to be led out *into the wilderness* and on into the promised land. *The valley of Achor* was the place where, according to the story of the first settlement, a member of the Israelite community committed the sin of concealing booty taken in battle instead of destroying it as instructed (Josh. 7). The result was that Israel suffered a heavy defeat until the offender and his immediate family had been eradicated. On this second occasion the place of disobedience and disaster will become *a gate of hope*, for Israel *will respond* with the kind of faithfulness which their ancestors had shown on their departure from Egypt. When this takes place Israelites will not even pronounce the name *Baal*. The word could simply mean 'husband' (as in Ex. 21.3, 22 etc.) but would cease to be used even in this sense because it was the name of the Canaanite god. Instead they would stick to the other word for *husband* which simply meant 'man'. This section also is closed with the formula *This is the word of the* LORD.

The future envisaged in these verses is a kind of 'second exodus', a recapitulation of the deliverance from Egypt. Now it is in the words of the exilic prophet preserved in Isaiah 40–55 that we meet with this idea and there it concerns the return from Babylon (Isa. 40.3; 48.20–21; 51.9–11). We have seen that the third section ended in v. 13 with a concluding formula and that the fourth section begins in v. 14 with a connecting word 'that is why' which had been used before but which has nothing to which it may refer here. The phrase *speak words of encouragement* (v. 14) is exactly the same expression as is found in Isa. 40.2, where REB has 'speak kindly'. All these factors point to the conclusion that vv. 1–13 were words of Hosea which warned and threatened judgment on Israel, but that vv. 14–17 were added when the words were remembered later to assure Judah of the impending return of the exiles from Babylon. Again, we are faced with the apparent paradox that God is the righteous one who judges sinners and also the loving one who rescues his people. Both views are found throughout scripture and must always be held in tension.

The covenant of Yahweh with Israel

2.18–23 The theme of a hopeful future is continued in the remaining verses of the chapter. Verse 18 speaks of *a covenant . . . with the wild beasts . . .* The word *covenant* is that which came to be used to describe the relationship between YHWH and Israel and it was characterized by peace. Here it is a bond between the people of Israel and the animal kingdom which will ensure a time of peace (cf. Isa. 11.6–9, where the reign of the coming king will do the same). The peace will extend to all human relationships since every *weapon of war* will be broken (cf. Isa. 2.4). All this is in the active voice. They are things which YHWH will do. This happy future is the outcome of neither chance nor human effort. It is due solely to YHWH. Picking up the marriage metaphor which Hosea had used so widely, the passage next takes up the theme of YHWH's relationship with Israel (v. 19). He will *betroth* Israel to himself, and the bond which will hold them together is *righteousness, justice, loyalty and love: he will make them faithful. Righteousness* means the fulfilment of obligations inherent in a relationship (see note on HONESTY at Amos 2.6); *justice* is the framework of behaviour which is constructed by this; *loyalty* is the quality best expressed by our word 'devotion'; *love* is derived from the same root as the word 'womb' and indicates 'compassion'; *faithful* describes a person whose fidelity holds him firmly within a relationship. With these qualities shown by YHWH and given by him to his people, they will *know* him as their God (see on 4. 1–8). All these are very familiar terms in the Old Testament. Hosea himself used them, as we shall see, but so did many others. Whoever was responsible for these verses was well versed in the language of relationships and perhaps followed Hosea's practice of using it. YHWH will not turn a deaf ear to his creation. When *the heavens* ask for rain or sun he will *answer*, and the process of asking and answering will permeate all creation. The name *Jezreel* will regain its positive significance of prosperity and plenty, and the other two children's names will be reversed. So Hosea's threats are balanced by these later promises.

'The faithless partner'

3.1–5   The main question to be answered about this chapter concerns its literary genre. As we have seen, it looks on the face of it to be a straightforward autobiographical account coming from Hosea himself. If we accept this answer, then some other difficult questions follow which scholars have answered in different ways.

First, who is the woman upon whom he must *bestow* his *love* (v. 1)? Many assume that it is Gomer, the same woman to whom he was married in ch. 1.[3] But this woman is *loved by another* man and is *an adulteress*. If this is Gomer, we should have to assume that she and Hosea had separated after the third child was born and that she had gone to live with another man. That may be so, of course, but

---

[3] J. L. Mays, *Hosea*, pp. 54 ff.

nowhere are we told so. It would still leave open the question as to why Hosea had to buy her back. Would that mean that something more than a separation had taken place, that there had been a more formal divorce and that somehow she had come into the legal possession of another man? Again, we are not told that this was so, nor are we aware of the circumstances in which such an arrangement could take place. It should be noted that the position of the word *again* in v. 1 does not require the woman to be the Gomer of ch. 1. In fact the word *again* may qualify either *said* – 'the LORD said to me again' or, as in REB, *Go again*. It cannot mean *'bestow your love* again.'

Secondly, it has been suggested that both ch. 1 and ch. 3 are describing the same marriage, but from different points of view. In ch. 1 the emphasis falls more on the children of the marriage, whereas in ch. 3 it falls upon the nature of the marriage itself. But in ch. 1 Gomer is simply *an unchaste woman;* here she is *an adulteress.* The former implies that she was a loose woman, the latter that she had been married and, presumably, was now in an adulterous relationship. Even more strange is the fact that whereas in ch. 1 she had three children with no suggestion of delay, in ch. 3 Hosea is forbidden to have sexual relations with her, at least for some time. So this solution raises as many problems as it solves.

Third, it could be that Hosea is being told to marry a different woman, this time *an adulteress.* This would not only shock any who saw it; it would put him in a very awkward position *vis-à-vis* the law, for it would involve him too in the crime of adultery. There would also arise a further question: if Gomer in ch. 1 represents Israel whom does the adulteress of ch. 3 represent? What message would the marriage be proclaiming? Could she represent Judah? If so, what would the story mean?

Fourth, if both chapters are allegorical the position is no better, for the analogy ought to make sense.

All these difficulties stem from regarding ch. 3 as autobiographical. But in fact we are quite used to stories written in the first person which are not autobiographical at all but where first-person narrative is simply a literary device or convention. This convention existed also in the ancient world, and the memoirs of Nehemiah are probably another example of it. Stories in the first person have been called *memorabilia.*[4] In such narratives a story which is meant to convey

---

[4] Cf. H. W. Wolff, *Hosea,* p. 57.

some truth is woven around a known fact in the life and experience of a well-known figure. Hence it is not entirely fictional, but neither is it wholly historical. There may have been a Robin Hood who had a band of followers, but the stories that are woven around him are meant to teach the lesson that the poor need care even if it means robbing the rich to provide it. This may not be an exact parallel but it may illustrate the kind of story we find here in ch. 3. The writer, who knew of Hosea and his marriage, tells a story based on that event, but for a new and different purpose, namely to warn the people of Judah not to follow the path taken by Israel. It is significant that in Jer. 3.6–11 a comparison is made between 'apostate Israel' who was 'less to blame' and 'that faithless woman Judah' (v. 11), and the whole passage is written in terms of marriage and adultery. The story here in ch. 3 speaks of *an adulteress* and not simply of an unchaste woman as in ch. 1. The word *love* occurs several times in v. 1. The Hebrew word is found, of course, in the rest of Hosea, but it is mainly used in Deuteronomy and in later books of the Old Testament. The phrase *other gods* is also a common Deuteronomistic phrase while the curious word for *cakes of raisins* is found elsewhere only in the Deuteronomistic history (II Sam. 6.19) and its parallel in I Chron. 16.3. Much of the language and many of the ideas, then, were current in the seventh century BCE. Most commentators regard the reference in v. 5 to *David their king* and the introductory phrase *after that* as coming from a Judaean editor and some regard the whole of v. 5 in that light. The detail of the price paid, *fifteen pieces of silver, a homer of barley, and a measure of wine* has sometimes been taken as a sign of authenticity. Various suggestions have been made about this price. It may have some reference to the value of a slave-girl gored by an ox – thirty shekels – half paid in cash and half in kind, (Ex. 21.32) but this is very uncertain. In any case a good story-teller would be likely to use such a description to show vividly how much trouble his hero had taken to buy his wife. It is best, then, to take ch. 3 as a coherent whole but to see it as a later Judaean story based on the fact of Hosea's marriage, but with the intention of showing how Judah is more guilty than Israel and yet God will take Judah back as his own after their punishment. *The Israelites*, a term not used elsewhere by Hosea, and here referring to the chosen people of God, rather than the Northern Kingdom, will live *without king* and without cult *for a long time*, as they did during the Babylonian exile; but then God will raise up a new David and the people will turn back to him and be restored as they are brought home again.

Interpreted in this way ch. 3 carries no message of hope for Northern Israel coming from the lips or activity of Hosea. It is a condemnation of Judah on account of its worship of Assyrian gods, probably in the reign of Manasseh, followed by a promise of restoration and a period of trial and then full restoration. All this was common enough among prophets like Jeremiah and Ezekiel.

We are now in a position to take stock of the situation with regard to this first part of the book of Hosea. The first three chapters undoubtedly form a coherent whole and were intended to do so by the person or persons who put all the material together in its present form. Within that coherent whole it is possible to discern the message of the prophet Hosea himself and also certain adaptations of his message to the situation in Judah somewhat later. It has been argued that the message of the prophet was very similar to that of Amos, though couched in different terms. The infidelity of Israel was such that judgment upon the nation was assured and Israel would lose her status as the people of God. This would leave her open to attack and defeat. Later events proved him right, for Israel was defeated by the Assyrians in 722 BCE and the kingdom came to an end (cf. 1.4). For his words to have been preserved at all they must have been carried by him or by others into the Southern Kingdom of Judah. Since his prophecies against Israel had been fulfilled, his words would be respected and they could be used by others to criticize Judah. They, however, added their own material based upon what Hosea had said and done. Judaean prophets like Jeremiah and Ezekiel certainly believed that Judah, too, would be punished for its disloyalty to YHWH but were convinced also that there was a future for Judah beyond that. Indeed they believed that Israel and Judah would be united again under a new king, a new David. This is repeated in passages like 1.10–11; 2.14–17 and 3.1–5. Finally, when Judah was defeated by the Babylonians and its leaders taken into exile, the final 'edition' of the book was made and hopes of a return comparable to the exodus from Egypt were included (2.18–23), similar to the hopes expressed in Isaiah 40–55. The hopes of a new David and a united Israel did not materialize after the exile. The inhabitants of the former Northern Kingdom, the Samaritans, were looked down upon by the Jews and there remained hostility and suspicion between the two. The hopes, however, were not diminished but were pushed into the future. Christians who look back on all this through the Jesus event see in him the fulfilment of this hope – the Christ, the Messiah, the new David – and regard the Christian community as the new Israel brought into being through his life, death and resurrection. So Peter could take up again the hopes expressed in Hosea and apply them to the Christian church (I Peter 2.10).

The Lord's case against Israel

Hosea 4.1–9.9

The opening of the case

4.1–3   The rest of the book of Hosea is made up of a collection of prophetic sayings and we hear no more about his life or activities. It begins with what looks like a 'motto' oracle introducing the theme of the whole collection (cf. Amos 1.2 and Isa. 1.2–3). It takes the form of a legal disputation and consists of a call to *hear* in v. 1, the charge in the second half of v. 1 and v. 2, and the judicial sentence in v. 3. Some think this 'form' was borrowed from a special legal ceremony connected with the Feast of Tabernacles, when annually or every seven years the law was read and the people judged against it (Deut. 31.9ff.). On the basis of an acknowledgment that they had broken it and that it was now binding upon them for the future, the covenant was renewed. The apparent references to the Decalogue in v. 2 may support this view. It is equally possible, however, that the procedure was well known both in the main centres where legal cases were judged and in the less formal gathering of the elders of a town or city to maintain justice there (cf. Amos 5.10).

The charge against Israel is spelled out in two ways, first in general and then in more specific terms. *Good faith* and *loyalty* are those very qualities which YHWH had promised to show to his people through Moses (Ex. 34.6) and which were therefore required from his people both to him and to one another. Psalm 12 similarly complains that these qualities are not to be found in Israel. Next comes *acknowledgement of God*. REB has translated the same word in v. 6 as *knowledge* and it would probably have been better to have done so here. The word is especially important for Hosea. It means more than intellectual awareness and probably more than *acknowledgement* as we normally use that word. It often carries with it an idea of intimacy and close relationship (cf. Amos 3.2). If there was no 'knowledge of God' in Israel it means that by failure to show *good faith* and *loyalty* they had spurned their proper relationship with God.

KNOWLEDGE OF GOD

Since the idea of 'knowing' is so common in Hosea it may be helpful at this point to examine it more closely. The verb 'to know' in Hebrew has a wide range of meanings. It was thoroughly investigated by the late Professor D. Winton Thomas in a number of articles and studies.[1] The variation of meaning is so wide that it may be there are two identical Hebrew roots with different meanings, one meaning 'to know' and the other meaning 'to humble' or 'to humiliate'. There are places like Gen. 4.1, where the meaning clearly is 'to have intercourse with' (REB 'lay with'), in which it is hard to decide which of the two roots is being used, always supposing there are two.

To begin with, 'knowledge' can and often does refer to the acquisition of information and the cerebral processes involved in that. An illustration of the verb's use in this simple sense may be found in II Sam. 11.20 ('You must have known . . .'). In the book of Proverbs the noun 'knowledge' is used fairly frequently as a parallel to 'understanding' or even 'wisdom' (cf. Prov. 14.6), where it refers not only to the information acquired but also to the process or the ability to acquire it. Then too, as in English, the verb may be used with a person as its object. Sometimes it merely means 'to be acquainted with' someone; sometimes it denotes a deeper relationship, 'to be familiar'. Unless it is derived from the second root meaning 'to humiliate', the sexual usage mentioned above is a vivid use of the word in this sense of being familiar. All this means that the exact connotation of the words, both verb and noun, has to be decided in the light of the context in which it is used. In v. 6 of this chapter, where the context is the teaching of the priests, it most probably means knowledge of the law, i.e. intellectual, mental awareness of its demands. Similarly in 9.7 and 11.3 it refers to knowledge of certain facts. But in v. 2 of the present

[1] See the bibliography of his works in *Words and Meanings: Essays presented to David Winton Thomas*, ed. P. R. Ackroyd and B. Lindars, Cambridge University Press 1968.

chapter, where *God* is the object, it possibly means more than awareness or recognition of God and is used of the relationship with him which ought to exist if only people showed *good faith* and *loyalty*. The familiar relationship which ought to be the mark of the chosen people no longer exists. In 5.4 it is this same relationship which is broken or prevented by their sin. The same meaning is found in 6.3,6; 8.2; 13.4.

4.2 sets out some specific ways in which the lack of *good faith, loyalty* and knowledge of God is manifested. *Kill, rob and commit adultery* are all deeds forbidden in the Decalogue in Ex. 20.13–15. To *swear oaths and break them* or to swear them with no intention of keeping them is close to 'taking the LORD's name in vain'. These particular wrongs are probably examples of a complete breakdown in social order in which acts of *violence* resulting in the frequent shedding of *blood* were commonly experienced. These sins were punishable not just because they were breaches of the law. The law was a guide to living in *good faith* and *loyalty*, and failure in respect of the law was simply a sign of a more fundamental malaise, namely the lack of all those qualities which held YHWH's people together.

The judicial sentence in v. 3 is introduced by the usual *Therefore* and is directed against *the land* and therefore against *all who live in it*. It will affect also the wildlife, for all living things depend on the fertility of the land, which the Israelites thought was provided by Baal (2.5) and which YHWH, the true giver, would withdraw (2.9). As remarked on 2.18, there is a bond between humanity and nature. The fortunes of the two are inseparable (cf. Gen. 3; Isa. 11; Rom, 8.15ff.).

The case against a priest

4.4–6 If vv. 1–3 are a 'motto' oracle they lead naturally into this next passage which is highly critical of the priests whose duty it was to teach the law to the people. Part at least of the reason for the people's disobedience was the failure of the priests to fulfil this responsibility. The Hebrew of v. 4 is difficult to understand but REB has probably caught the right meaning, though it involves some slight change in the text of the third line. The court case with which the collection has opened is not one brought by a human being, not even by Hosea himself; it is brought by YHWH who addresses his people through his prophet and his *quarrel* is largely *with the priest*. *The priest* is addressed in the singular. Whether it refers to the priest in charge at Bethel (cf. Amos 7.10–16) or some other one in, say, Samaria we cannot say. It could just possibly be used in a collective sense. In the second line of v. 5 Hosea mentioned *the prophet* alongside the priest. Since he criticized prophets nowhere else, some commentators have been inclined to omit this line as a later comment recalling, for instance, the confrontation between Jeremiah and Hananiah (Jer. 27.28). But there had been and probably still were false prophets in Israel (I Kings 22). Moreover the actual word order of the Hebrew suggests that lines one and two are parallel and, further, the prophet, like the priest, was responsible for making known the mind and purpose of God. Literally, the last line of v. 5 should be translated 'and I will destroy your mother'. This is extremely unlikely to be what Hosea meant. There is a rare word very similar to the word for 'mother' which means 'people' or *nation*, and REB is doubtless correct to follow this meaning, especially as the last line of v. 5 is then parallel with the first line of v. 6, leaving two more parallel lines in v. 6.

As was stated above, *knowledge* in v. 6 seems closer to mental grasp than to relationship with God. The *people* have lacked adequate *knowledge* of God's will and have come *to ruin*, but it is fundamentally the fault of the *priest* who had *rejected knowledge* and *forsaken the teaching* (Hebrew *tôráh* sometimes means 'law'). Therefore YHWH will *reject* him and *forsake* his children. Thus there is a serious warning here for all those in positions of leadership whose responsibility it is to pass on to their people the message of God concerning the way they live their lives. Ezekiel makes a similar point when he describes the prophet as a watchman (Ezek. 3.16–21; cf. Hosea 5.8).

Priests and people devoid of understanding

4.7–14 This section again begins with an attack on the *priests*, moves on to include both *people and priest* (v. 9) and then seems to be critical of the whole people. It is clear from v. 7 that Hosea is not critical of

the priesthood as an institution. It is an office which carries with it
dignity, a word sometimes translated 'honour' or 'glory'. It is the sin
of the priest which causes him to *turn their dignity into dishonour*.
Here, however, the sin is not limited to one priest but to the
priesthood of Hosea's day as a whole. In v. 8 the verb *batten* is used
in the sense of 'grow fat on'. RSV's 'greedy for' is perhaps closer to
the Hebrew. The verb means that the priests welcome it when the
people sin and are anxious for it to happen more often because it
means more sacrifice and, since they share the offered meat, more
food for them. Verse 9 seems to extend the punishment to both *people
and priest*, yet the word *eat* in v. 10 looks as though it is picking up
the *feed* of v. 8 (it is the same word in the Hebrew) and that may
suggest that v. 10 refers only to the priests. REB seems to understand
this with its *resort to prostitutes*. The word is usually translated 'play
the harlot' and naturally the subject is usually feminine. The only
place where a man is the subject of the verb is in Num. 25.1, and this
is during an incident to which Hosea refers again later (9.10). There
it refers to participation in the Canaanite sexual orgies, and so it is
quite likely that here it refers to the priests sharing in the Canaanite
fertility rites; but their union with cultic prostitutes will produce no
offspring. This accords well with the fact that *they have abandoned the
LORD* (vv. 10c–11a).

The rest of the passage (vv. 11b–14) certainly seems to refer to the
whole people and not just to the priests. The *wine* which *steals my
people's wits* may be either wine drunk at parties or wine used to
excess in Canaanite religious rites as is suggested by vv. 12 and 13.
The mockery of seeking *advice from a piece of wood* reminds us of the
prophet of the exile who also makes fun of idolatry (Isa. 40.18ff.;
44.9ff.). To be fair, those who worshipped idols did not usually
believe that a piece of wood was a god, but rather that the spirit or
god lived in the wood. Still, the mockery is effective. Canaanite
shrines were often situated on *mountain tops* and *terebinths* were
sacred trees. In Hosea it is never easy to be sure whether *promiscuity*
(v. 12) refers to activities within the cult or to activities in life generally
or, metaphorically, to Israel's attitude to YHWH. Similarly although
v. 14c and *d* refer to cultic prostitution, vv. 13e and *f*, 14a and *b* may
refer to sexual irregularities outside worship, encouraged by what
went on inside. Interestingly this section dealing with the whole
people begins with those whose *wits* were stolen (v. 11) and ends

with *people devoid of understanding*, (v. 14), making what is sometimes called an 'inclusio'.

The dangers of false worship

4.15–19 While this passage deals predominantly with *Israel* or *Ephraim*, one of Hosea's favourite names for the Northern Kingdom, the second line of v. 15 refers to *Judah*. It is unlikely that Hosea warned the people of Judah against visiting the shrines at *Beth-aven* and *Gilgal*.[2] We should probably regard the line as an addition made when the prophecy was being used later in Judah. The warning to the Israelites not to visit these shrines echoes similar passages in Amos (4.4; 5.4f.) but the reason is different. Here it is connected with *adultery* – again we cannot be sure of what kind. In any case no good can come of it. *Beth-aven* (house of 'wickedness' or 'idolatry') is surely a nickname for Bethel (house of God). Two similes are combined in v. 16. *Like a heifer Israel has turned stubborn*, i.e. they will not turn to worship him; *will the Lord now feed them like lambs?* The answer expected is 'No', but the question reminds us of Isa. 40.11. Verses 17 and 18 offer some very difficult Hebrew but REB has made the meaning as clear as possible. The drunkenness and *immorality* have the same ambiguity as mentioned above. The drunkenness picks up v.11, the *immorality* vv. 13–14, the preference for *dishonour* rather than *glory* v. 7 and the *sacrifices* v. 13. The result of all this is that *the wind will carry them off*. There can be no doubt that Hosea attacked all the practices of Baal worship. Perhaps it was not so much that Baal had displaced YHWH as that the Israelites were worshipping Baal as a kind of insurance in case YHWH could not cope with the provision of fertility. Perhaps it was that they intended to worship YHWH but were doing so as though he were Baal. Perhaps they were tempted by the attractiveness of the wine and sexual excesses. It is not always clear which, and perhaps the degree of syncretism or idolatry varied from person to person, from group to group. For Hosea, however, there could be no other God for Israel than YHWH and anything

---

[2] Again, cf. Emmerson, *Hosea*, pp. 120ff.

associated with Baal was anathema. Good faith, loyalty and know-ledge of God were lacking and so their *sacrifices* will be a *delusion*. It will not save them; *the wind will carry them off*. So, Hosea calls us to undivided loyalty to YHWH, whom we now know as the Father of Jesus, who also said 'No one can serve two masters . . . You cannot serve God and money' (Matt. 6.24).

The withdrawal of Yahweh

5.1–7   This oracle was addressed to three groups of people, *priests, Israel* and *the royal house*. It is perhaps a little strange that while the first and third groups are the leadership of Israel, the second is *Israel* itself. In fact, the Hebrew has 'house of Israel'. The same phrase is used in Micah 3.1 where it is parallel with 'leaders of Jacob' and where REB has translated it 'rulers of Israel'. There is every reason to think that in this present passage also it refers not to all the people but to the leadership. *Sentence is passed on you* may equally well mean 'Justice is your responsibility' and a very similar phrase, again in Micah 3.1, is translated by REB 'It is for you to know what is right'. The leaders of Israel had the responsibility for seeing that right prevailed in the land. There then follow three hunting metaphors, *a snare*, a trap and *a deep pit*. This suggests that the leaders were allowing things to happen at *Mizpah, Tabor* and *Shittim* which were leading the people into the sin of idolatry or syncretism. *Mizpah* probably refers to a town in the territory earlier occupied by the tribe of Benjamin (Josh. 18.26) and there was an important shrine there. The Israelites gathered there to punish the Benjaminites for the rape of a Levite's concubine by the young men of Gibeah (Judg. 20.1ff.) and also to meet Samuel, who acted as judge there for a ceremony of repentance so that the Philistines should not overcome the Israelites (I Sam. 7.5). Mount Tabor was an isolated hill in the valley of Jezreel from which the Israelites swooped down to defeat the Canaanite king of Hazor (Judg. 4). There was probably a shrine there (Ps. 89.12) which may have been associated with the royal palace in Jezreel. *Shittim* is the place where the Israelites camped at the point of entry into Canaan (Num. 25.1) and where they shared in the sexual orgies of the people of Pe'or (Hos. 9.10). Hosea often did look back to ancient traditions such as these, but it is more likely that here he was referring to practices in the immediate past which the Israelite leaders had encouraged at shrines in these places and for which YHWH would now *punish them all*. Whereas the leaders had trapped Israel into sin, YHWH himself had *cared for Ephraim* (the verb is literally 'known' again). Now all Israel *has become promiscuous* and *brought defilement on himself*. Hosea used the sexual metaphor once more to describe the people's worship of Baal. In the strongest terms he asserted that there was no *way back to their God* (v. 4). Their sin *barred the way* (literally 'does not allow them to return'; 'Return' is another favourite word of Hosea) and prevented them *from knowing the Lord* (cf. 4.1). So the LORD 'knew' them; they were disloyal and therefore now they could not 'know' the LORD. Later passages such as 6.1–3 have to be understood in the light of this strong statememt. In the following verse (5) the line about *Judah* is extra to the parallelism and again reflects the re-use of Hosea's words in that kingdom. So, when Israel did *go to seek the LORD* i.e to worship him, and sacrifice at the shrines (cf. Amos 5.4), they would *not find him*. They had forfeited the right of access they should have had into his presence. In fact, his presence was denied them, for he had *withdrawn from them*. The God who 'knew' them had now left them, for they had *deceived* or betrayed him. Consequently without his help and protection *their fields* were wide open to the depredation of *an invader*. The word for field often refers to the 'portion allocated' and would recall that the *fields* had been promised and granted to them by YHWH.

The oracles contained in 5.8–6.11 were probably spoken during the time of the so-called Syro-Ephraimite alliance (see Introduction) and collected here because of that common background. The threat to the western states from Assyria under Tiglath Pileser III became very severe about 735 BCE. Syria and Israel entered into an alliance in an attempt to withstand it and they sought to involve Judah as well. Judah was reluctant to join partly because the threat was less severe on account of its geographical situation, partly because according to II Kings 16.6 Judah was under pressure from Edom in the south and partly because Ahaz, a twenty-year-old, had just become king. Syria and Israel therefore jointly attacked Judah and besieged Jerusalem (under their kings Rezin and Pekah) with a view to replacing Ahaz with a king more amenable to their plans. We have an account of the same events from a Judaean perspective in Isaiah 7 and 8. It should be said that Hosea never made explicit reference to any of these things; it is rather that these oracles which do involve Judah take on a sharper meaning if they are seen against this background.

The watchman's warning

5.8–15   In vv. 8 and 9 Hosea spoke as a watchman (cf. Ezek. 3.17f.) warning against invasion. The three towns to which the warning is addressed, *Gibeah*, *Ramah* and *Beth-aven*, all lay in the territory traditionally allocated to *Benjamin* and Ephraim. *Benjamin* was the most southerly district of the Northern Kingdom on the border with Judah. The towns are named in a south to north order and therefore were stages along the route an invader from the south might take. *Beth-aven* may refer to a town of that name or it may be a nickname for Bethel as in 4.15. In any case, if Hosea, as watchman, warned towns along that line and promised support to *Benjamin*, it is much more likely that the attack was expected to come from Judah and not from Assyria, since Assyria would be more likely to attack from the east or north. Judaean sources such as the books of Kings and Isaiah make no mention of such an attack by Judah on Israel and it may well have been that none materialized. After all, this was only a warning. Hosea knew that a *day of punishment* had been *decreed for Israel's tribes* and thought it might be through an attack by Judah. *This is the certain doom I have decreed,* though it catches the meaning of the Hebrew, is rather too strong. 'Among Israel's tribes I have made known what is sure to happen' is closer to the Hebrew, and it was through Hosea that YHWH had done so.

In vv. 10–12 both nations, *Ephraim* and *Judah*, were condemned, *Judah* because the *rulers* had been moving *their neighbour's boundary*. The practice of moving boundary stones in order to steal some of a neighbour's land was forbidden by the law and carried with it a divine curse (Deut. 27.17). Judah and Israel were neighbours not only in the sense of occupying adjacent territory but because both were part of the people of God. The appropriation of Israelite territory was an offence against a fellow member of the people who had been given and allocated their respective territories by YHWH. That is how Hosea saw it. Just as individuals would fall under the divine curse, so *Judah* would experience the *wrath* of God in full *flood*. But *Ephraim* is in no better case. The words *oppressor* and *trampling* are actually in the passive voice in the Hebrew and RSV has translated them so; 'Ephraim is oppressed, crushed in judgment.' It makes much better sense, though, to treat them as active, which REB has done. The main charge against Israel, however, was that she was *obstinately pursuing what is worthless*. This is not the word used elsewhere to denote idolatry. It is a different word, used in Isa. 28.10 and translated 'meaningless noise' and is a reference to a worthless ally, Syria. Both nations would therefore suffer divine judgment. The events of 735 BCE turned out badly for both nations. Far from discouraging the Assyrians it encouraged them to attack the Northern states so that Damascus was captured and much of Israel annexed in 732. Meanwhile the fact that Judah sought the help of the Assyrians against the coalition meant that it would fall under the domination of that nation. This is reflected in v. 13. In REB it reads as though it was *Ephraim* who *sent envoys to the Great King*, but it is likely that lines 1 and 3 refer to *Ephraim* and 2 and 4 to *Judah*. This preserves the parallelism, and since no subject is expressed in line 4 it could very well refer to Judah. Certainly, as just stated, Judah did seek help from Assyria, and *the Great King* is the title given to the Assyrian king. That *Ephraim turned to Assyria* is less certain, though it is possible that Hoshea did so by 732, for the Assyrians then made him king. In neither case was it any use. The king of Assyria was powerless to deal with the problems of both nations. The punishment of both is likened to an attack by a wild animal and reminds us of Amos (cf. Amos 1.2; 3.12 etc.).

5.15 connects vv. 8–14 with what follows in ch. 6. First, Hosea indicated where the fault lay. They had not sought YHWH either in worship or in the conduct of their international affairs. Second, he stated the consequences. YHWH would *return* to his *dwelling place*, leaving them alone and unprotected as in v. 6. Third, this situation would continue *until* in genuine repentance they turned to *search* for him. The word *remorse* is really a verb meaning 'to acknowledge guilt'. The root is that from which the name of the guilt offering is derived and it carries the idea of restitution. The *search*, therefore, must be no superficial activity. It will involve recognition of guilt and a readiness to do all that is necessary for a meeting again to take place. To this we shall return in the following verses.

We must beware of regarding passages like ch. 5 as encouraging a policy of isolationism in international affairs. It may be that the prophets' prohibition against alliances with foreign nations is their vivid way of stressing the need for total trust in YHWH. It may be, too, that they recognized that such alliances carried religious implications since submission sometimes meant official recognition of the strong nation's gods. In any case we must be careful not to make general inferences from particular situations. Hosea was not giving a lecture on international affairs, he was passing on what he believed to be God's word to Israel in the situation in which the nation found itself in 735 BCE. What remains of enduring significance and value is not so much what he forbids as what he enjoins – trust in and fidelity towards God, whose will must be sought and obeyed in all circumstances.

Israel's shallow repentance

6.1–11a

6.1–3   At first sight this suggests that the people were now beginning to *search diligently* for YHWH, for this is their response to Hosea's message and apparently they wish to *return to the LORD*. It is, however, a flawed response. In the first place v. 1 expresses the all too easy assumption that all they have to do is *return*, and God will reverse his attitude towards them. They do not seem to have grasped that *their misdeeds have barred their way back to God* (5.4) and there is no sign of the *remorse* which was required in 5.15. *Dieu pardonnera: c'est son métier* – 'God will forgive: that's his job' – seems to have been their attitude. The whole passage is therefore shallow. Secondly, what at first looks like supreme confidence proves to be nothing more than arrogance. God is bound to respond and bring the bad times to an end. The conjunction of the phrases *on the third day* and *he will raise us to live* . . . at once brings to the minds of Christians the resurrection of Jesus and the promise of the risen life for the believers. It has to be said, however, that originally this had nothing to do with

125

resurrection. Israel was *torn* and *wounded* but not yet dead. If the whole context of this passage was the aftermath of the Syro-Ephraimite alliance, when a large part of Israelite territory had been annexed by Assyria, the words *torn* and *wounded* take on a specific meaning. *Raise us to live in his presence* therefore does not mean that God will bring Israel back from the dead as a nation. Life is not simply a matter of breathing: it involves blessing from God and prosperity (see note on Amos 5.4–6). Sickness such as Israel was experiencing metaphorically was death drawing its victims downwards towards Sheol. What Israelites were looking for and believed they could acquire by returning to the LORD was a complete reversal of their fortunes. They wanted to live in the presence of God, which is the highest blessing of all, but they wanted it on the cheap. Another life-giving blessing in Canaan was *the rain*, and they have a facile belief that God will be *like the rain*. He will refresh them and this is as certain *as the sunrise*. Again the emphasis is upon their own effort, *Let us strive*, or 'pursue' *to know the Lord*. Perhaps their pursuit of this full and intimate relationship with God was through the cult, in which case the passage comes close to the word of Amos in 4.4f. They were right to seek the LORD, to return to him, to want to know him. What was lacking was a sense of *remorse* for their sin. Without that sacrifices, worship, or even will-power could not achieve the relationship they hoped for. Until they were confessed and dealt with *their misdeeds* still *barred the way back to God*. There is no such thing as 'cheap grace' as Dietrich Bonhoeffer called it. 'Cheap grace is the teaching of forgiveness without requiring repentance, baptism without church discipline, communion without confession, absolution without contrition.'[3]

6.4–6 YHWH's reaction to this shallow attitude was one of puzzlement. How could he possibly open their eyes to what they were doing? As in the earlier passages, Hosea was still concerned with both kingdoms, *Ephraim* and *Judah*, the whole people of God. Any *loyalty*, any devotion which seemed momentarily to have stirred within them had vanished like the *morning mist* and *dew*. Anyone who has visited Israel, in the summer especially, will know that that is very quickly indeed. *That is why* introduces not a future judgment as is usually the case, but one which has already begun. *I have cut*

---

[3] Dietrich Bonhoeffer, *The Cost of Discipleship*, SCM Press 1948, Macmillan, New York 1949, p. 39.

them to pieces by the prophets does not mean that the *prophets* actually took up the sword, of course. It was *my words*, which he had made known through *the prophets*, that did the damage. We do not know who *the prophets* were that Hosea was referring to. Some of them he had already condemned (4.5). Elijah and Micaiah seem to be too far in the past, for Hosea seems to have been speaking about recent disasters. Did he know about Amos? Quite probably there were others too, whose words have never been preserved. Their relationship with YHWH is here made clear. They were instruments of his will and they helped to bring about what he purposed by speaking the word which he had given them. The battle language would have reminded the people that traditionally YHWH gave victory to Israel over Egyptians and Canaanites alike. In Ex. 14.14 at the sea and in Josh. 6 at Jericho Israel had to do nothing in the way of fighting. God fought for them (see on Amos 5.18). Now the situation was reversed. YHWH had fought against Israel (cf. Isa. 28.21, where this is a 'strange' or alien work) and had taken part of the promised land which he had given them out of their control.

It is in the light of what has gone before in vv. 1–3 and 4–5 that we are to read and interpret v. 6. It is one of those verses in the prophets dealing with sacrifice which seem to deny its value (cf. Isa. 1.10; Jer. 7.21; Amos 5.21f.; Micah 6.6).[4] There are two ways of translating and interpreting the verse and they depend on the meaning given to a small Hebrew preposition. First, we may follow the translation in REB. Then the first line is quite clear except that *require* would be slightly better translated as 'am pleased with' or 'take pleasure in'. So YHWH is pleased with *loyalty* (cf. 4.1; 6.4) and is not pleased with *sacrifice*. The second line says something rather different: he is more pleased with *acknowledgement* or 'knowledge' (see note on 4.1) *of God* than with *whole-offerings*. The first line states a contrast and the second a comparison. We should then regard the second line as a modification of the first, explaining that it is not really a question of either-or; it is a strong way of saying that *sacrifice* without *loyalty* is worthless. Secondly, we may translate the second line as: knowledge *of God* without *whole-offerings*. This has the effect of retaining the contrast in both lines and would suggest that YHWH does not want sacrifices, but he does want a relationship in which his people are

[4] Cf. H. H. Rowley, 'The Meaning of Sacrifice in the Old Testament', *BJRL* 33, 1950–51, pp. 74–110, reprinted in *From Moses to Qumran*, Lutterworth Press and Association Press 1963, pp. 67–107.

wholly devoted to him. Of the two interpretations the first is more likely to be correct. It is difficult to believe that any of the prophets could envisage a religion without sacrifice (cf. on Amos 5.21–24). Moreover, this fits the context better. The sequence of ideas in the whole section seems to be as follows. Because of their conduct during the Syro-Ephraimite alliance when they had failed to trust YHWH he had announced his departure – *I shall return to my dwelling-place* (5.15). Israel had thought to *return to the Lord* (6.1) but too superficially and without the necessary *remorse*. They imagined that if they reverted to the outward forms of worship of YHWH he would have no alternative but to allow them into his presence and provide them with blessing and life. YHWH, aware of this shallowness and the evanescence of their expressed *loyalty*, responds by reminding them that *sacrifices* without an enduring *loyalty* and 'knowledge' *of God* are quite unacceptable to him. This means that Israel and Judah both remain separated from him. *The way back to their God* is *barred* by *their misdeeds* (5.4) and they are still under judgment.

6.7–11   This passage draws attention to some incident in the past which characterized Israel as sinful and apostate, a condition in which she still remained. The difficulty is in identifying the incident. *Admah* is mentioned again in 11.8 in association with Zeboyim and both cities are linked with Sodom and Gomorrah in Gen. 10.19; 14.2, 8; Deut. 29.23. This would suggest that it was situated in the area of the Dead Sea. The rest of the passage, however, deals with Gilead and Shechem and so it is unlikely that this is the place intended by Hosea, and if it is a place name we have to say that we have no information now as to what happened there. In fact, the text does not say *At Admah* but, as REB's footnote makes clear, 'Like Adam'. Now 'Adam' simply means 'man' in the sense of 'mankind' and therefore the phrase may simply mean 'as men do'. The *they* is emphatic and we should translate the line *'They, as men do, violated my covenant'*. The word *there* in the next line does not then point backwards to *Admah* but forwards to *Shechem* in v. 9. The word *there* in v. 10 also points towards *Shechem*, for as REB footnote points out, there is no mention of *Bethel* in the Hebrew text.

All this makes interpretation difficult, but it seems more than likely that we should be looking for some incident at *Shechem* and the one that comes to mind is Abimelech's attempt to establish a monarchy at Shechem, supported by the Baalites (Judg. 6–9). There are, in fact, many verbal connections between the text in Hosea and the story in Judges (for more details see additional note). If this is the incident referred to, then it fits well with two major themes in Hosea's preaching, the monarchy and Baalism. It need not be a polemic against the monarchy as an institution, but against a monarchy supported by idolatry and apostasy.

THE COVENANT AT SHECHEM

Covenant (v. 7) and *Shechem* (v. 9) are connected in two ways. First it was here at Shechem that Joshua was said to have renewed the covenant first made at Sinai (Josh. 24). Second, the Canaanite god worshipped there was known as Baal-berith, meaning 'Baal of covenant' (Judg. 9.4). Abimelech's monarchy there was supported by money from the sanctuary of Baal-berith. It was therefore a violation of the YHWH covenant renewed by Joshua. *They played me false* is not a very common word but it is found also in Judg. 9.23, where REB translates 'broke faith with him'. In the Hebrew text *Gilead* is described as a 'town' or 'city' *of evil-doers*. Now Gilead was not a city at all but an area east of the Jordan. There is, however, a genealogical link between Gilead as an individual and Abimelech, and also between Gilead and Shechem (Num. 26.30 ff.). Gilead was descended from Joseph through Manasseh and Machir (cf. also Josh. 17.2). From Gilead were descended Shechem and Jeezra or Abiezra. Now in Judg. 6.11 Gideon is described as an Abi-ezrite and as belonging to the clan of Manasseh. The use of *Gilead* by Hosea is therefore not out of place, even though it lies in Transjordania, for it is connected in tradition with Shechem and the story in Judg. 9. *Trail of blood* may then be a reference to Abimelech's slaughter of his seventy brothers in Judg. 9.5. He was supported by the inhabitants of Shechem (Judg. 9.6) but the word translated 'inhabitants' by REB is *ba'alîm* and they were possibly priests or leaders associated with Baal-berith, the god of Shechem. Verse 9 of the present text therefore refers to the events in Judg. 9.25, 32, where the '*ba'alîm*', inhabitants of Shechem, lay in wait around the city. Hosea 6.10 should read 'in the house of Israel *I have seen a horrible thing*'. *There Ephraim became promiscuous* (or 'played the harlot') would be appropriate enough, seeing that Abimelech was supported by Baal worshippers. In the view of some he himself was a Canaanite, being the son of Jerubaal, who was later identified with the Israelite Gideon. All these correspondences are sufficient to make it very likely that this was the episode Hosea was referring to as he condemned contemporary Israel for similar wrongs.

Although the passage as a whole seems to refer to Israel exclusively it ends with a warning also to *Judah*. This may be a later addition like others we have noted, but there is really no reason why Hosea should not have included *Judah* at the end of the oracle, seeing that both nations together are addressed in the preceding section beginning at 5/8. It then rounds off the collection of sayings from the period of the Syro-Ephraimite alliance and its aftermath.

Failure of kings and princes

6.11*b*–7.7 The final line of ch. 6 clearly opens the saying in 7.1–7. The phrase *restore the fortunes of my people* (cf. Amos 9.14) later came to be used of the return of the Judaean exiles from Babylon. It probably had its origin in the New Year rite, which celebrated the restoration of fertility with the coming of the rains following the dry summer months. By extension this meant a change of fortunes for the people as well and it came to be used not only in the sphere of nature but also in the realm of politics. It contains one of Hosea's favourite words, 'to return'. The parallel line contains another, *to heal* (cf. 5.13; 6.1; 14.5), which denoted YHWH's readiness to forgive and restore his people to wholeness, their present disturbed condition being regarded as sickness (5.13). However, each time the possibility of such a change entered Hosea's mind, it seems to have been countered by the awareness of Israel's sin, which made it impossible, for *they have not kept faith*. This is less vivid than the Hebrew, which speaks of them performing deceitful actions that give the lie to the special relationship Israel was supposed to have with God. Burglary and muggings were rife, but it never entered their minds that YHWH *had in mind* (literally 'remembered') *their wickedness*. So they were trapped by *their misdeeds*, which God could see around them even if they could not. In v. 3 REB uses the word *divert* in the sense of 'to amuse' – they make the king merry. By a very slight change in the Hebrew text some commentators translate this 'they anoint the king'. Although this might be tempting, in view of Hosea's attitude to the monarchy, it is not necessary. Nevertheless, even if we retain the word *divert*, it does seem from v. 5 that the coronation of a new king was in mind and this may well have been King Hoshea, who was placed on the throne by the Assyrians in 731 BCE. In the previous dozen years there had been coup after coup as Zechariah, Shallum, Menahem, Pekahiah, Pekah had reigned briefly and then been overthrown (see on 1.1). The rejoicing which should have accompanied the coronation was still there but it was brought about by *wickedness* and *treachery*. Three times in the following verses Ephraim is compared with an *oven* which is *heated* by *fire*. The Hebrew text is so difficult that it is hard to see what the point of the comparison is. Verse 4 mentions *adulterers* but, as often, it is unclear whether this refers to actual sexual misconduct or whether it is used metaphorically of Israel's infidelity. The *oven* was a large cone-shaped clay structure. It was heated by lighting a fire on the floor of it. When it was hot and the flames had died down the dough could be put in to bake. Quite probably the baker would stir up the fire while the dough was rising to get maximum heat. Verse 4 would then suggest that their desires were so 'hot' that they didn't even need any stirring. Verse 5 suggests that on the coronation day *the courtiers* made themselves ill (this is the literal meaning behind *become inflamed*) *with* the potency of the *wine*. These excesses of sexual and drinking activity have suggested to some that *their king* refers to Baal, but in the light of v. 7 it is more likely to refer to the new king of Israel. Verse 6 reverts to the baking metaphor, where it is not sexual passion but intrigue which was hot within them. The Hebrew text, however, does not speak of them as being *heated* but as 'drawing near'. The word *intrigues* comes from a root meaning 'to ambush', here used figuratively. If we were to transfer *their hearts* and *like an oven* to the following line then 'they draw near with their intrigues' would be left to follow nicely after *he himself joins with arrogant men*. This would leave v. 6 with just the metaphor 'their heart is like an oven.' *Their passion* requires yet another alteration to the Hebrew, which reads 'their baker'. It is better to retain the Hebrew and read:

> They draw near with their intrigues
> Their heart is like an oven

> During the night the baker sleeps
> But in the morning it burns like a blazing fire

7.7 also continues the metaphor of the *heated oven*, this time in connection with the change of king, which is probably the *intrigue* or ambush mentioned in v. 6. The last line of v. 7 is the crucial one. Revolutions, coups, changes of monarch may in certain circumstances be permissible (cf. I Kings 11.29ff.; 19.15–17; II Kings 9) but only when YHWH said so. Here they have been carried out without reference to him at all (cf. 8.4). Morever, when those chosen became king they did not *call to* YHWH either in gratitude or for help. In other words the political situation had become divorced from religion, with God being left out of account altogether.

Futility of alliances

7.8–12   Not only did Israel ignore YHWH in matters concerning the monarchy; they ignored him also by making alliances with foreign nations (cf. 5.13ff.). The two topics were, of course, connected, especially since Hoshea was a puppet king imposed by Assyria. In the twenty years or so between the rise of Tiglath Pileser III in c.745 BCE and the fall of Samaria in 722, Israel alternated between Assyria and Egypt besides making an alliance with Syria. It is this liking for alliances which Hosea refers to in the metaphor, not this time of the oven, but of the bread baked in it. Being *mixed up* with foreigners like flour and water, Ephraim finished up *half done*. Far from being any help to Israel the various allies had taken advantage of them but they had not the sense to see it. *Grey hairs*, old age, were supposed to bring wisdom, but Israel had failed to see what was happening. Their *arrogance* in ignoring God testified against them and *they do not return to the Lord* (cf. 5.4). Nor do they even try.

Hosea then turned to another metaphor to illustrate the folly of foreign alliances. Israel flitted from one nation to another like *a silly senseless pigeon*. King Menahem had paid tribute to Assyria (II Kings 15.19); it is possible that the Syro-Ephraimite alliance expected some help from Eygpt. Hoshea was certainly pro-Assyrian and was a vassal but he apparently withheld tribute and sought help from Egypt

(II Kings 17.4). *Like birds*, therefore, YHWH would *bring them down* and hold them *captive*. As in the previous passage it was not so much the making of the alliances which Hosea criticized, but the failure of trust and loyalty towards YHWH which such alliances revealed.

Evil plotted against Yahweh

7.13–16 This passage, too, may well come from the period when Hoshea was approaching Egypt for help. Here again the real issue was their *rebelling against* YHWH. This is the same word as that found in Amos 1 and 2 and there translated 'crime'. The contrast between YHWH's attitude towards them and their attitude to him is brought out strongly in the Hebrew by emphasizing the *I* and the *they*. *I*, for my part would *deliver them*, but *they*, for their part *tell lies about* or against *me*. This doesn't mean they tell lies to other people about YHWH but rather that all they do and say in worship is a lie. So, in v. 14, *there is no sincerity in their cry to me*. This *wailing and gashing of themselves* reminds us of the prophets of Baal on Mount Carmel (I Kings 18.28). These actions showed just how much they were treating YHWH as a Baal. That is the essence of their lie. Their behaviour in all this was not to turn to YHWH but to *turn away* from him. In spite of all the *support* he had given them they had now fallen back into their *useless worship*. As the footnote in REB shows, this is the probable meaning of some unintelligible Hebrew. When they *fall by the sword*, i.e. were defeated in battle, the Egyptians to whom they had turned for help would make fun of them.

Again we are bound to ask whether this chapter advocates both political isolationism supported by trust in YHWH and a society in which there should be no king because God alone is King. It could be interpreted in this way (see note on 5.13). Two points need to be made, however. First, Hosea was not seeking to lay down universal principles which are applicable to all ages; he was dealing with a concrete situation in Israel in his own day. Therefore we have to look for underlying principles, such as an overriding trust in God, which needs to be applied to all circumstances of life. Secondly, this was probably not what Hosea meant anyway. Whether it be in the choice of kings or a decision about allies, what mattered for Israel was that they should be obedient to God's will because they were his chosen people. It can never be a question of doing what we want and then seeking God's blessing on it but of listening to God in worship or through his servants to discover his will and to trust him as we seek to do it.

Kings and idols

8.1–6   The first six verses of this chapter raise a number of interesting points. The passage is presented in the form of a 'call to arms'. The opening call is in the singular, as is the word trumpet in Hebrew (though REB has *trumpets*) and this has led some to think that it was Hosea himself who was commanded to sound the alarm. However, the prophet was probably using a well-known stereotyped phrase which he had taken over in its familiar singular form to introduce his divine threat. The *eagle* doubtless stands for Assyria. *The sanctuary of the Lord* is literally 'the house of the LORD' and most probably refers to Bethel – the house of God. Perhaps Hosea deliberately avoided using Bethel because 'El', who should be equated with YHWH, had become confused with Baal. He is therefore describing the *sanctuary* as it should be. The people have *violated* the *covenant* (cf. 6.7). T. C. Vriezen defines *covenant* as an encircling bond binding YHWH and Israel together.[5] To violate it (literally 'to cross over') is thus to pass outside the circle. *Covenant* is not much mentioned in the eighth-century prophets, and here it stands in parallel with *instruction* or law (*tôrāh*). This does not mean that the two words are exactly synonymous but that their meaning is close enough for the two to be used together, the one expanding or more closely defining the other. The phrase 'violate the covenant' and the association of 'covenant' with 'law' are found often in the Deuteronomic writings (Deut. 17.2; Josh. 7.11,15; Judg. 2.20; II Kings 18.12), the former frequently referring to the worship of other gods. This raises the question of the relationship between Hosea and Deuteronomy. Clearly there was some connection between the two, though its nature is uncertain. Was Hosea familiar with those who produced

---

[5] T. C. Vriezen, *An Outline of Old Testament Theology*, Blackwell 1970, p. 168.

the book of Deuteronomy? Or are the similarities due to the compilation and editing of the book of Hosea by the Deuteronomists? Or was it common language of the day with which both were familiar? It is hard to say, but if the Deuteronomic movement had its origin among Israelites from the Northern Kingdom roughly at the time of its fall in 722 BCE, and Hosea was still at work shortly before that event, then such connections are perhaps not all that surprising.

As in 6.1 Hosea again quoted what people were saying: this time *We acknowledge you as our God* or, better, 'My God, we know you' (see note on 4.1–3). This singular pronoun in the Hebrew may suggest that the words were those of a priest representing Israel. The assertion indicates their mistaken belief that they had some automatic claim on God irrespective of their behaviour. To 'know God' is exactly what Hosea had been calling for and what he saw to be lacking. He was convinced that they did not 'know' him and their claim to do so simply underscored their arrogance. The *good* which Israel *rejects* remains undefined. The word has as wide a range of meaning in Hebrew as it does in English. It is tempting to wonder whether the word has some special connection with YHWH at Bethel, for in Amos 5.14 the prophet speaking at Bethel, calls on people to 'Seek good' whereas in 5.4 he said 'Seek YHWH'. It may then be a rejection of YHWH himself and all that he could give. So, in spite of their assertion *an enemy pursues* them.

8.4–6 tell us more precisely what was wrong; it again concerns the monarchy and the cult, those two matters Hosea so frequently deals with. Having said that, some uncertainty remains about the meaning of *they make kings*. The difficulty lies in the fact that *they make kings* represents just one Hebrew verb which means 'to be king' but is used here in a causative form meaning 'they caused to be king', and we cannot be sure whether it refers to one king or to many. If with REB we translate as referring to the plural *kings*, then the verse would almost certainly be an indictment of the rapid succession of kings following the death of Jeroboam II (cf. the remarks on 1.1). All these changes took place without reference to YHWH. The tense of the verb, incidentally, is almost certainly perfect or past tense. Suppose, however, the verb refers to making a king in the past. It may then be understood as referring to the crowning of Jeroboam I. There may be some support for this view from the fact that in the following verses Hosea was critical of the *calf-god* which the same Jeroboam I had placed in the shrine of Bethel. So it may be that Hosea was looking back to the beginnings of the Northern monarchy and cult. The difficulty with this view is that Jeroboam was not made king *without divine authority*. The account in II Kings 11.28ff. says he was promised the kingship by the prophet Ahijah. Curiously the Deuteronomic historian, who had not a good word for Jeroboam I or his successors and regarded his monarchy as apostasy, still records this. He did not, however, mention any anointing or any charismatic gifts, as in the case of David, or even the Northern king Jehu at a later date. This may have been quite intentional, though we dare not build too much on an argument from silence. In any case we have already seen in 1.4–5 that the name of Hosea's first son was a condemnation of the dynasty of Jehu in spite of the fact that he had been promised the kingdom by Elijah and anointed by Elisha or one of his disciples. So Hosea may have felt just as critical of Jeroboam I as he was of Jehu, even though a prophet had promised him the throne. It may be then that Hosea found himself opposed to the Northern monarchy as an institution. It would be possible to go even one stage further and to say that Hosea aligned himself with the view expressed in I Sam. 8.4–22 that the very institution of monarchy was an act of rebellion against the kingship of YHWH. What is certain is that he opposed the more or less contemporary succession of kings and it may be that his opposition went deeper, to the whole line of Northern kings, or even to the very idea of monarchy itself.

This is coupled with the other main fault of Israel. The monarchy was supported by idolatry. Verses 5–6 almost certainly refer to the golden bulls which Jeroboam I had set up at Bethel and Dan (I Kings 10). There is a clear connection between these and the making of the golden calf in the wilderness (Ex. 32), which we cannot explore more fully here. There is little doubt, however, that Jeroboam never intended these as idols, but as pedestals for YHWH, just as was the case with the Ark in Jerusalem. After the separation of the North from the South in 922 BCE access to the Ark in the Jerusalem Temple was denied to the people of Israel, and some such substitute was essential in the shrines there. It is significant that Amos, although he prophesied at Bethel, never condemned the bull. This suggests that even in his day it was not regarded as an idol, but by the time of Hosea and Deuteronomy it clearly was. The process was doubtless helped by the fact that Baal was sometimes represented as a bull. It seems then that both king and bull, necessary as they may have been, were seen by Hosea as man-made institutions and therefore an an affront to YHWH.

8.5, then, threatens the destruction of the calf but suggests that the *calf-god* was in Samaria in apparent contradiction to what has just been said about the bull being at Bethel. We know from I Kings 16.32 and II Kings 10.5.ff. that there was some sort of Baal cult at Samaria, which had been built as the capital of Israel by Omri in the ninth century. It is possible that, as he developed the capital, his son Ahab included a bull to correspond with those at Bethel and Dan. However, according to II Kings 10.26 Jehu completely destroyed everything to do with the cult there and it remained deserted 'to this day', that is, to the time of the composition of II Kings during the exile. So it is unlikely that there was a bull there in the days of Hosea. Archaeology has uncovered no sign of a shrine containing a calf-image. It is possible, then, that *Samaria* refers to the people and not to the city. The people at court there probably worshipped at the royal shrine (cf. Amos 7.13) in Bethel. In 10.5 also *the inhabitants of Samaria tremble for the calf-god of Beth-aven* (Bethel). The singular *calf* may suggest that Dan, where the second bull had been placed, had already been occupied by the Assyrians, as it was in 732 BCE. In any case Dan never seems to have played as important a part as the royal shrine at Bethel.

The *how long?* of v. 5 expresses a sense of hopelessness, for Hosea could not imagine a time when Israel would be innocent. *The calf was made in Israel* is an attempt to translate a Hebrew phrase which literally means simply 'far from (or, apart from) Israel'. This may, in fact, be the completion of v.5 and mean that because of their persistent guilt the present people had become separate from the true Israel. It is worth recalling that Bethel, where the *calf-god* was established, was the shrine associated in tradition with Jacob (Gen. 28), whose name was later changed to Israel (Gen. 32.28). Hosea made use of these traditions in ch. 12 and they may have been in his mind here. The Israel which he knew was far removed from the Israel which Jacob became. Although the *calf* is not mentioned in the Hebrew of the first line of v.6 it is clearly intended by the pronoun *it*, which stands in a quite emphatic position at the beginning and end of the first two lines and then is defined at the end of the verse.

> It a craftsman has made
> And no god is it;

> For splinters it shall be,
> The calf of Samaria.

This ridiculing of idols reminds us of the exilic prophet (Isa. 40.18–20; 44.9–10). Actually, it is unlikely that the ancient peoples confused the idol with the god. Rather they believed that the god took up residence in the idol. But the chance of such confusion made the ridicule more telling (cf. 4.12).

The trouble with Israel's national and religious institutions was that they had no support from God and were the product of human minds and hands. All 'ecclesiastical institutions' have to be judged in this light.

Sowing the wind
8.7–14

8.7–10 It would appear from this saying that the prophet was speaking after 732 BCE, when much of Israel had come under direct Assyrian rule and the rest was governed by Hoshea, controlled by Assyria. It opens with a proverbial saying which, in slightly, more familiar form, is found elsewhere (Prov. 11.18; 22.8; Job 4.8; II Cor. 9.6; Gal. 6.7). Normally it promises a harvest in keeping with what has been sown; here it promises much more; *Israel sows the wind and reaps the whirlwind*. Whether *the wind* which *Israel sows* refers to the self-reliance which Hosea attacked in the previous verses or to the dependence on Assyria which he mentioned in the following ones (vv.9 and 10) is hard to say. The second part of v.7 also seems to be based on a familiar saying, but it has been expanded by Hosea, who introduced the *strangers* who would *swallow up* any *heads* which should happen to appear on the *standing grain*. Already the process of *swallowing up* Israel had begun and what was left was regarded as being *of no value*. Next, Hosea used the simile of *a wild ass* which went about *its own way* without any control to describe Israel's readiness to submit to Assyria and pay the price. *Ephraim has* paid the price for her love affairs (v.9). The consequences of this which follow in v.10

are far from clear. A meaningful translation can be obtained only by making some changes to the Hebrew text. REB has understood the verse to mean that Israel will be forced to give up the monarchy altogether, presumably because of its total loss of independence. This happened, of course, in 722 BCE. Different changes produce a different meaning, for example, 'I will assemble them (for judgment) and they will soon writhe under the burden imposed by the king of rulers (i.e. the king of Assyria).' In other words their subjection will become even more severe. Though we cannot be sure precisely what Hosea intended, it is clear that he envisaged a severe punishment, even more severe than the proverb of v.7 in its usual form would suggest.

8.11–13 In these verses Hosea returned to his favourite theme of worship, but not this time to accuse the people specifically of Baal worship. The complaint is set out in vv.11–12 and the announcement of judgment in v.13. First, they have greatly increased the number of altars and therefore sanctuaries. Just as the Deuteronomists came to believe that sacrifice should be offered only 'at the place where the LORD shall cause his name to dwell' (Deut. 12.11) so perhaps Hosea, too, saw the dangers attendant on the multiplicity of places for sacrifice where it would be all too easy for people to engage in practices unacceptable to YHWH. In any case they had been *occasions for sin* (cf. Amos 4.14). Second, they treated the written law as *irrelevant*. This need not refer to any particular collection of laws presently found in our Old Testament, though it would be tempting to think of some collection based on the Decalogue (cf. 4.1) and similar to that in Deut. 12–26. It may, of course, refer to a collection of written laws concerning sacrifice, but already in 4.8 Hosea had complained of the neglect of the law and its exposition by the priests. Probably a similar point is being made here. All the emphasis was being placed on the human activity of making sacrifices, and the more the merrier (cf. 4.9), without any corresponding attention being given to the Word of God given in the law. The judgment in v.13 is expressed as Hosea's own words with *the* LORD referred to in the third person. He would *not accept* their sacrifices, some of which, if offered in the right spirit, should have provided a channel for divine forgiveness. Instead *their guilt will be remembered* and *their sins punished*. The verbs are active, not passive, and have YHWH as their subject. 'To remember' always means more than just 'call to mind'; it carries the implication that God will act upon what he recalls. The ultimate punishment is a return to bondage, figuratively in *Egypt*, literally in Assyria. *To go back to Egypt*, however, would also suggest that the whole direction of Israel's history was to be reversed and her special relationship with God abrogated.

8.14   It is not easy to see the connection of this verse with either what has gone before or what comes after. The fact that *Israel* had *built palaces* suggests a much more settled and prosperous time than that envisaged in the previous verses. If it is a saying of Hosea himself, we should have to locate it in the earlier part of his ministry. It may have been placed here because it appears to deal with mistaken priorities. This time they have *built palaces* instead of 'remembering' YHWH and putting their trust in him. This may refer in an oblique way to the monarchy (cf. 8.4), or it may denote prosperity, or even fortifications. A similar charge is laid against *Judah*, unless we regard this as a later comment by a Judaean using Hosea's prophecies in the Southern Kingdom. Whatever they rely on, *cities* and *citadels*, they will be destroyed. There are, however, some reasons for thinking that the whole verse could belong to a later period. First, Hosea nowhere else spoke of YHWH as Israel's *Maker*. The exilic prophet responsible for Isa. 40–55 fairly frequently described YHWH as Israel's creator and on four occasions used the word 'Maker' (45.9,11; 51.13; 54.5) and in 51.13 uses this phrase almost exactly: 'Why have you forgotten the LORD your maker?' Secondly, the last two lines are almost identical with the judgment on the foreign nations in Amos 1.3–2.5, including the one against Judah. From whatever source the verse comes, it serves as a warning against forgetting, almost 'ignoring' God, and relying on things which, on the face of it, look strong and safe. The God who brought his people into being alone has power to help and save; other sources of confidence will be removed.

A joyless festival

9.1–9   These verses form a single unit although the last three appear to have a different subject matter. Verse 5 makes it clear that they have to be seen against the background of the Feast of Tabernacles, the great autumnal festival which celebrated the fruit harvest of grapes, olives and figs. Indeed it is likely that Hosea spoke these words while the festival was in progress at Bethel. This feast was the most important of the three pilgrim feasts to which, according to the law, all Israelite males were to go each year (Ex. 23.17). Since they were pilgrim feasts, i.e. feasts to which people travelled, they were held in the main religious centres, Jerusalem in Judah, Bethel and Dan in Israel. So important was this particular one that it was sometimes referred to simply as 'the feast' or, as here, 'the feast of YHWH'. Almost certainly a similar festival was celebrated by the Canaanites prior to the settlement of the Israelites in Canaan. The Israelites continued the practice but instead of being celebrated in honour of Baal it was now a feast for YHWH. Its importance lay not only in the fact that the fruit harvest had been or was being gathered, but also in the need to seek, from Baal in the case of the Canaanites but from YHWH in the case of the Israelites, rain to put an end to the summer season and to make possible the fertility of the land in readiness for next year. Another feature of the feast associated with the giving of rain was the recognition of YHWH as King (cf. the later Zech, 14. 16–19). It was called the Feast of Tabernacles or Booths, according to Lev. 23.43, because the Israelites lived in booths in the days of the wilderness wanderings. This is not strictly true, for there they lived in tents. 'Booths', on the other hand, were temporary shelters consisting of four upright poles with a roof of leaves and branches. They were erected in the fields and vineyards when the harvest was being gathered to provide shelter from the heat of the midday sun. We have already seen (2.8f.) how Israel was tempted to give thanks to Baal as the giver of fertility and harvest, instead of recognizing these as gifts from YHWH.

Rejoicing was obviously the keynote of the festival. As might be expected the word *rejoice* does not occur frequently in the earlier prophetic books because, by and large, the prophets saw little to rejoice about. It is, of course, common in the Psalms, which were used in worship. Here, therefore, Hosea forbids the people to *rejoice*. In spite of the keynote of the festival they had nothing to *rejoice* about since they had been *unfaithful* to their God. Hosea again uses the sexual metaphor. The harvest which they saw before them led them to worship Baal, not YHWH. The consequence of this follows in v.2. Those very fruits would not be available to them, for they would be removed from *the Lord's land*. They had been behaving as though it were Baal's land. Hosea affirmed that it was *the Lord's*, and therefore they would be excluded from it. They would *go back to Egypt*, not literally but metaphorically, as in 8.13. The history of the chosen people would be reversed: out of the promised land *back to Egypt*. Literally, they would be removed into parts of the Assyrian empire, as they were in 722 BCE, and the *food* they would be forced to eat there would be *unclean*. Although REB translates the verbs in v.4 as though they were prohibitions, there is no reason why they should not be understood as simple futures (so RSV). In the foreign lands to which they would go they would not be able to *pour out wine to the Lord* or make *pleasing sacrifices*. This *food* would not first be offered in sacrifice but would be eaten just to keep them alive. It would not be *offered in the house of the Lord* because this, presumably Bethel (cf. 8.1), would no longer be accessible to them. Therefore at the time of the Feast of Tabernacles they would be completely at a loss with no opportunity to celebrate. Verse 6 envisages that some may flee literally to Egypt, to escape the *devastation* wrought by Assyria, but it would become their tomb. Their belongings and their homes would be lost among *weeds* and *thorns* as they were left untended.

9.7–9 reiterate the punishment which Israel must undergo, but the verses also deal with the question of the prophet and his role. Israel, to whom Hosea spoke, knew very well that the time had come, though some commentators understand this to mean 'Israel is humiliated' (see note on 4.1). *The prophet has become a fool* may just possibly be Hosea's estimate of those court prophets who ought to have been watchmen but instead allowed Israel to fall into the *trap* of idolatry. It is more likely, however, that he was quoting the people's estimate of himself as they responded to his scathing condemnation and threatened punishment. They regarded him as *a fool* and *a madman*. *The inspired seer* is a translation of a phrase which literally means 'a man of spirit' and which recalls passages like I Sam. 10.9, when the spirit of God took hold of Saul and he began to prophesy. The phrase means a man possessed with divine power. We cannot deduce from this anything about the style of Hosea's prophesying, whether he was an ecstatic prophet or not. The emphasis is rather on his message, to which people reacted by saying he was crazy, as crazy, perhaps, as the ecstatic prophets whom Saul temporarily joined. What had driven Hosea to say such outrageous things that people regarded him in this light was their *great guilt*. The precise meaning of the first line of v.8 is uncertain but the important part of it is indisputable, *the prophet* was *a watchman for Ephraim*. This was Hosea's own perception of his role, and we have met two passages already where he has functioned in this way (5.8ff. and 8.1ff.). As noted there this view of the prophet was dealt with at greater length by Ezekiel (Ezek. 3.17ff.; 33.1ff.). Because of their unwillingness to hear the warning of the *watchman* he has become *a trap* to catch them in their sin. Consequently he has fallen foul of the officials at the sanctuary, *the very temple of God*, literally, 'the house of his God' (Bethel) (cf. Amos 7.10–16). *The time of Gibeah* to which Hosea referred again in 10.9 probably refers to the incident recounted at length in Judg. 19–21, in which the rape of a Levite's concubine by the men of Gibeah almost led to the extermination of the tribe of Benjamin. Israel's present sin is as bad as that, and deserving of a similar punishment.

God's judgment on Israel
Hosea 9.10–13.16

Israel's first contact with Baal

9.10–17 We have already seen how on a number of occasions Hosea made reference to the past traditions of Israel, for the most part (e.g. 6.7–11; 9.9) recorded in the Old Testament. From this point in the book onwards this is even more noticeable; so much so that this may be regarded as the beginning of a new section of the book in which sayings of this kind have been gathered together. So as we examine the next few chapters we have to be aware of stories dealing with Israel's past. This present passage (vv. 10–17) falls into two distinct parts, one dealing with the sin at *Baal-peor* (vv. 10–14) and the other with *wickedness at Gilgal*. Both parts follow exactly the same formal pattern – a reference to past tradition (vv. 10 and 15), a word of judgment against Israel spoken by YHWH to his prophet (vv. 11–13 and 16) and the response of the prophet to YHWH (vv. 14 and 17). The whole is a conversation between YHWH and his prophet on two closely related subjects. It may be that such a conversation was made necessary by the opposition Hosea encountered in vv. 7–9. At any rate that is the way it is presented to us by the book in its present form. Such conversations form part of the vision reports in Amos 7.1–9; 8.1–3, and are found in Jeremiah (12.1–13; 15.15–21). The conversation about *Baal-peor* begins with YHWH reminding his prophet of the beginnings of the relationship between YHWH and Israel and says two things about it. First, it was miraculous; *grapes* do not grow *in the wilderness*; YHWH and Israel did not meet by chance or accident. Second the meeting was a great joy to YHWH, as great as that of a traveller who *came upon . . . grapes in the wilderness*. We need to use our imagination to appreciate the *joy* which YHWH experienced. Elsewhere Hosea spoke of Israel's beginnings in Egypt (2.15; 11.1; 12.9; 13.4) but the wilderness tradition was also important to him, since it was there at Sinai that the covenant was made and the Decalogue given (Ex. 19–24; Hos. 2.14). So the wilderness was an ideal time. Curiously he did not mention the incident of the golden calf (Ex. 32) and this is perhaps surprising in view of his condemnation of the *calf-god* (8.5). The event which changed YHWH's joy into sorrow and anger was a different incident. As they approached the promised land they came to *Baal-peor*. The story of what happened there is told in Num. 25 and referred to in Deut. 4. 3. In fact, two things are said to have taken place. First, Moabite girls enticed Israelite men and persuaded them to 'join in the worship of Baal of Peor' as REB puts it. More literally, they 'yoked themselves' to him (Num. 25.3). Hosea chose an even stronger word, *they consecrated themselves*. The verb he used is that from which the name Nazirite is derived (cf. Amos 2.11). The Israelites gave to Baal the kind of allegiance which the Nazirites gave to YHWH. Whether it was through a non-religious orgy or through the sexual activities associated with Baal worship that the Israelite men were enticed we cannot be sure, but the latter is likely, for Hosea regarded these beliefs and practices associated with Baal as at the heart of Israel's problems. In Num. 25.4 the punishment was to be 'hurled down to their death in the broad light of day' (REB). The second incident in Num. 25.6–9 concerns an Israelite man who took a Midianite girl into his tent, where they were discovered in the act of intercourse. In this case the punishment was that a priest drove a spear through them both as they lay together. Hosea made no mention of either of the punishments. It was clearly the cultic involvement with Baal which concerned him, for it provided him with an early example of what was now wrong with Israel. The present sin is therefore of long standing. For Hosea the consequence of this sin was that the Israelites had become *as loathsome as the thing they loved*. That people tend to become like whatever they worship is true generally. The punishment which Hosea heard from YHWH was all the more telling because of the sexual nature of Baal worship. Their *honour* or 'glory' certainly included offspring but it would *fly away like a bird*. No children would be born, nor even be carried in the womb, nor even be conceived. If by any chance some children were born they would not be allowed to live. To be *without posterity* had a dreadful finality about it, for the only way in which people in Old Testament times could think of living on beyond death was through their reputation and their children. All this punishment would come about because YHWH would have turned *away from them* (cf.4.6; 5.6). In v. 13 the Hebrew of the first line is virtually untranslatable. The nearest one can get to a literal translation would be 'Ephraim, as I have seen, is for Tyre shoots planted in a meadow', which makes no sense at all. REB, like all other translations, has to assume changes in the text. Since in Ps. 83.12 the promised land is called 'God's meadow', it is just possible that the line originally made some reference to Israel's settlement there. Whatever it means, the verse as a whole continues the theme of punishment. Verse 14 is then the prophet's response. As translated in REB, Hosea simply acquiesced in what YHWH had said, but RSV is better here: 'Give them, LORD – what will you give?' In other words Hosea probably began to make intercession (cf. Amos 7.2, 5) What he was going to ask we shall never know, for he realized the futility of intercession and felt compelled to agree with what YHWH had decreed.

The second part of this section (vv. 15–17) concerns some *wickedness at Gilgal* which *aroused* God's *hatred*. As we know from Amos 4. 4, *Gilgal* was an important shrine in the eighth century but the incident to which he refers here is not clear at first. It was the place where the Israelites first set foot on Canaanite soil (Josh. 4.19) and therefore it may have provided a parallel with *Baal-peor* as the place where they made contact with Canaanite life and culture, but there is no existing tradition in the Old Testament of any sin committed there. The next significant mention of *Gilgal* is in I Sam. 11.12f. as the place where Samuel, who acted as judge there (I Sam. 7.16), anointed Saul as king after his victory over the Ammonites at Jabesh-gilead. It seems as though there had been some resistance to his kingship, for in the euphoria of victory the victors wished to kill those who had opposed it. It seems likely, therefore, that the two things which Hosea believed to be Israel's fundamental errors are coupled together again – the Canaanite cult of Baal at Peor and the monarchy at Gilgal. In v. 10 they had become *loathsome*; here in v. 15 they have forefeited God's *love, for all their rulers* ('princes' rather than 'kings' though it may include both) *are in revolt.* The withdrawal of his *love*, just like the turning away from them in v. 12, results in their punishment, and this is similar to that described in v. 11. This time, in v. 17, Hosea made no attempt at intercession, but simply confirms the punishment in different terms. Like Cain the murderer (Gen. 4.12) they would *become wanderers among the nations* (see note on Amos 9.9), as indeed they did in 722 BCE.

The consequences of misunderstanding Yahweh

10.1–4   This section is rather unusual in that it is a saying spoken by the prophet himself in which both God and Israel are mentioned in the third person. We are therefore bound to ask to whom Hosea was speaking, but there can be no clear answer to the question. Perhaps it was some group of people who had shown sympathy and support for what he had been saying. More than that we cannot say. The content of its message is already familiar to us though Hosea finds no difficulty in expressing it in new ways. Here he likens Israel to a *spreading vine*. This reminds us of Ps. 80.8, which speaks of Israel as a vine brought out of Egypt and planted in Canaan, where it took root and spread until it filled the land. In the Psalm the wall has been broken down and the vineyard ravaged. Hosea does not press the metaphor quite as far as this. Rather he was concerned to show that as Israel settled in and spread out in Canaan they built more and *more altars* (cf. 8.11) and even better stone *pillars*. Such stone pillars were erected at Canaanite sanctuaries, where they represented Baal, but, according to Gen. 28.18, Jacob took the stone on which he had rested his head at Bethel, set it up as a pillar and poured oil over it. At the entrance to Solomon's Temple in Jerusalem were two large bronze pillars, Jachin and Boaz (I Kings 7.15–22), the meaning and function of which are unclear. Even if the *pillars* may legitimately be found in Israelite sanctuaries, Hosea now saw that they had become part of the apparatus of Baal worship. It may be thought proper and praiseworthy that the more prosperous they became *the more altars* and *pillars* they built for worship of the deity, but the first line of v. 2 suggests they had an ulterior motive. They were *false at heart* (literally 'their heart or mind was slippery'!). As J. L. Mays puts it, it was 'turning part of the profit back into the business'.[1] Their altars were not used to thank God but to secure further prosperity. Such a

---

[1] Mays, *Hosea*, p. 139.

misunderstanding of the nature of YHWH could only result in his destroying the *altars* and *pillars* they had built.

As so often Hosea turned from cult to monarchy. The verb in the first line may be either a present or a future. The fact that the Hebrew contains the word 'now' may suggest a present, and REB have understood it in this way: *Well may they say*. Then we have to ask at what period during Hosea's activity could the people claim, '*We have no king*.' It would have to be during an interregnum, and the most likely time would be between Pekah and Hoshea in c. 732 BCE at the time of the Assyrian attack on and annexation of much Israelite territory. They put this down to the fact that they failed to *fear the Lord,* i.e. show him the reverence, respect and worship which was his due. In their hopeless situation they felt there was nothing *the king could do for* them. Alternatively the 'now' in the Hebrew may point to some imminent occasion of punishment as in the previous verse. At that time the people '<u>will</u> say . . .' In this case the verse threatens the end of the monarchy when the Israelites would realize that this was due to their lack of *fear of the Lord* and there was nothing a king could do to help them, Verse 4 describes the failures of the king or kings in three very short phrases. First, 'they speak words', which REB rightly understands to mean that there is plenty of talk but no action. Second, they *swear oaths* which are empty and valueless and which would involve 'taking YHWH's name in vain' (Ex. 20.7). Third, 'they make a covenant', i.e. they enter into agreements, which may mean they enter into an agreement with their own people at their coronation but, again, the words are not supported by action. It may equally well mean that they make alliances with foreign nations. Finally in the last half of the verse they turn 'justice', or more narrowly *litigation*, into poison (cf. Amos 5.7) to such an extent that it spreads all over the fields, i.e. the land of Israel.

The end of the calf-god

10.5–8   In v. 5 Hosea turned back again to the shrine at Bethel and its *calf-god*. Like the monarchy this too will come to an end, being *carried away into exile* in *Assyria* while both *people* and *priests lament* its passing. Once more *Beth-aven* (house of wickedness) stands for Bethel (house of God) (cf. 4. 15; 5. 8 etc). The calf image would be part of the *tribute* money demanded by *the Great King*, the King of Assyria. It is difficult to understand how Hosea could have said Israel was *lacking counsel* or advice when he had himself been so eloquent in calling for a true and full 'return' to YHWH, a call which had been consistently ignored. Some versions have therefore amended the Hebrew text so as to read 'because of its idol' (RSV) 'because of disobedience' (NEB). If we are to retain the text and the translation of REB we should probably think of *counsel* as the advice given by the officials at court, a meaning it often has (cf. II Sam. 15.12 etc.).[2] So capital and *king, shrines* and *altars* will all be done away with. Left naked, they will call on the *mountains* and *hills* to *cover* them, a verse recalled by Jesus and applied to the leaders and people of Jerusalem after they had ordered his crucifixion (Luke 23.30).

Pictures of disaster

10.9–15 This section is made up of three smaller ones, all threatening disaster for Israel, the first (vv. 9–10) and third (vv. 13*b*–15) using military language, the second (vv. 11–13*a*) using the agricultural metaphor.

In vv. 9–10 Hosea again looked back to some sinful incident at *Gibeah*, presumably the same one as he had in mind in 9.9 when Benjaminites raped a Levite's concubine and attacked his family, an action which almost led to their extinction. In v. 10, however, he spoke of *two shameful deeds*. Since Israel's first king, Saul, was a Benjaminite who, according to I Sam, 10.26, had his home at *Gibeah*, the second shameful deed may refer to the institution of the monarchy. Where Hosea condemned the monarchy, however, it is not clear that his attack was on the institution, it may well have been on the contemporary kings, or even on the Northern kings whom he regarded as schismatic from the Davidic line. As we have seen already (cf. 8.4), it is difficult to reach a firm conclusion on this. We should remember, too, that Jeremiah spoke of Israel committing two sins

---

[2] W. McKane, *Prophets and Wise Men* (Studies in Biblical Theology 44), SCM Press 1965, pp. 55 ff.

(Jer. 2.13, where he meant turning away from YHWH and turning towards other gods). Hosea perhaps meant the same *two shameful deeds* here. The sin of *Gibeah* was not just an event buried in past history; it revealed an underlying propensity which persisted to Hosea's own day and which would result in military defeat. Such defeat was YHWH's doing; it was his chastisement of his people, who had rebelled against him. In one line it is YHWH who will *chastise them*, in the next it is the *peoples who mass against them*. The history of Israel may be looked at in both ways, as the outworking of human relationships and as the activity of YHWH. Modern history may still be viewed from both perspectives, as may an individual's life. For the Old Testament and for Christians they are not alternatives because God is the Lord of history. They are the two sides of the same coin.

10.11–13*a*   use agricultural imagery to illustrate Israel's persistent wickedness. In the early days Israel was trained and controlled by YHWH. They enjoyed their work. As the footnote shows, v. 11 also mentions 'Judah'. This is quite out of place in Hosea's original saying and this is why REB has omitted it from the text. It is important, however, for it reminds us again how the words of the prophet were still regarded as relevant to new and later situations in the other kingdom. The *yoke* under which Israel was to work in Canaan is defined in v. 12. This is not what God was saying to Israel of the eighth century through Hosea: it is the command given to Israel as the people settled in the agricultural land of Canaan. Not only were they to *sow* and *reap* grain; they were also required to show the qualities of life and behaviour which YHWH had first shown to them and then demanded from them, *justice* and *loyalty* (cf. 4.3). That was to be a *time to seek the LORD*, to worship and obey him until he should come and rain *justice* or possibly 'victory' (see note on Amos 2.6) on them. However, instead of this (v. 13) they have *ploughed, reaped* and enjoyed the very opposites, *wickedness, depravity* and *treachery*.

In the third section, vv. 13*b*–15, where we return to the language of war, the verbs are all in the singular. It may be that Israel was being so addressed, but it is more likely that this saying was directed to the king as the representative of his people. It was, after all, the king who was responsible for the defence policy which focussed on armaments to the exclusion of YHWH. The result of such a policy would be failure and disaster. We know nothing of the incident referred to in v. 14. There was apparently a Moabite called *Shalman* who is mentioned in Tiglath Pileser's Assyrian records but this is unlikely to refer to him and the Old Testament contains no other reference to the name. *Beth-arbel*, too, is mentioned only here. Presumably, Hosea was referring to some past tradition of which no record now remains. The *dashing* of *mothers and babes to the ground* or similar treatment is not unknown (cf. Amos 1.13; Hosea 13.16; Ps. 137.9), though sometimes a city and its surrounding villages could be described as mother and daughters. So *Bethel*, the royal sanctuary, and the *king* himself *will be swept away* as quickly as day breaks (cf. 6.4).

Throughout the chapter Hosea was concerned with the sanctuary and what went on there and with the monarchy and its behaviour. It is unlikely that Hosea envisaged an Israel in which cult and sanctuaries, kings, treaties and alliances were totally absent. It is more likely that he was critical of over-reliance on these to the exclusion of trust in YHWH. Without this essential ingredient the chosen people had no future, for the things they relied on would all be removed and Israel, left with no defence, would be destroyed.

God's love for Israel

11.1–11 This chapter is probably the best known and best loved part of the whole book of Hosea, for it speaks of God's love for Israel, Israel's rejection of that love, God's judgment on Israel and, in its final form, God's restoration and renewal of Israel. It is this last section which makes the chapter so appealing, for it is the first indication since ch. 3 that Hosea saw any future for Israel. In studying the chapter it is important to bear in mind that its structure is based on a legal procedure in which a father accused a son of rebellious conduct, as set out in Deut. 13.6–11 and, more pertinently, Deut. 21.18–21. If the case was proven the penalty was death by stoning. It may be questioned whether the death penalty was ever actually carried out, and we have no information about what punishment took its place. The metaphor of father and son for YHWH's relationship with Israel is a striking one for, like Hosea's other metaphor of husband and wife it could easily be misunderstood. It could readily have been taken to mean that God was literally the progenitor of his people in the way that some other gods were thought to have fathered their people. The relationship for Israel had its basis, of course, not in physical generation but in the choice of Israel by YHWH. Though the term is not used, 'adoption' would describe the relationship better. The idea was not wholly original or unique to Hosea. In Ex. 4.22 which, if the Pentateuch is to be divided into sources, comes from an early source, Israel is called YHWH's son at the time of his concern for the people in Egypt prior to the exodus. Isaiah also uses the metaphor in 1.2.

11.1–9 The motive behind YHWH's call *out of Egypt* is nothing other than the prior love of God. This is not the term sometimes translated 'loyalty'; it is the word which is used in a similar context in Deut. 7.7. Verse 2 quickly moves on to the time when they were in Canaan. The entry into the Promised Land was the point at which things began to go wrong (9.10, 15), for it was there they began to *sacrifice to the baalim*, ignoring the continuing call of YHWH. The *I* of v. 3 is quite emphatic. It was not Baal but YHWH who acted as father to Israel (cf. 2.5) but *they did not know* it – that word 'know' again (cf. 4.1, 6; 6.3; 7.9; 8.2, 4; 9.7; 13.4). The picture described in v. 4 according to REB is almost certainly what Hosea intended, though other translations do differ slightly. At Ugarit in North Syria many Canaanite texts and pictures have been found among which are some which show a father lifting a child to his chest as a sign of affection or perhaps to feed him. Hosea therefore described Israel as a child being brought up, nourished and taught to walk by its father. Such was the care YHWH bestowed upon Israel.

In vv. 5–7 the metaphor is left behind and punishment was directed against Israel for their refusal to behave as his children, for their failure to recognize him as the source of the good things they enjoyed, and for their rebellion against his authority. *Back to Egypt* is one way of describing it, a return to the condition they were in before YHWH *called* them *out*. (cf. 8.13). More literally they would come under the rule of the Assyrian king. They would 'return' *to Egypt* because they *refused to return* to YHWH; they were *bent on* 'turning away' (v. 7). REB *rebellion* is a good translation but fails to bring out the play on the word 'turn'. The first line of v. 6 is very graphic: 'a sword will whirl round in their cities' and the *sword* must be that of the Assyrians. There is some uncertainty whether the following two lines refer to the *priests* or to other elements in the cities such as the 'gate-bars' and 'fortresses'. Either translation requires some emendation of the Hebrew. Since sword is the subject of the verbs perhaps people are more likely to be their objects than things. The translation *priests* is still uncertain however, for the word really denotes 'empty talkers'. In Isa. 44.25; Jer. 50.36, REB translates the same word as 'false prophets' and it probably should be translated similarly here. *Scheming* represents a word which means 'advice' or 'plan' and is derived from the same root as *counsel* in 10.6. The verse, then, seems to be directed against those who have given advice to the king whether they be 'false prophets' or other courtiers. Although the word *Baal* does not occur in the Hebrew of v. 7 he is probably intended by a curious phrase which seems to mean 'high god'. This is better than RSV's 'appointed to the yoke'.

So far, then, the message has been one of utter defeat for Israel. Now in vv. 8–9, according to the usual translation, well represented by REB, YHWH changed his mind and decided not, be it noted, to destroy and then to restore Israel after punishment but actually to revoke the punishment on his son altogether.[3] This *change of heart* or mind is then explained by reference to the statement in v. 9 that YHWH is *God, not a mortal*. Therefore he is free not only to change his mind but to annul the penalty which he has laid down in his law for a rebellious son. So God wrestled with himself over the verdict he should pronounce and in the end his love prevailed over his justice. This is all very well and it comes as a relief after all the threats, but if this is what Hosea meant he was clearly wrong, for the punishment was carried out. Israel did come to an end in 722 BCE and the people were handed over to the Assyrians.

Attempts have been made to overcome the problem in different ways. Von Rad[4] suggests the possibility that the promise was made to the faithful who would be saved and the threats were addressed to the wicked who would be destroyed, but there is not a hint of this in the text. Others have argued that though Hosea was wrong historically the passage nevertheless gives an insight into the nature of God, and the promise was fulfilled in the New Testament in Christ. But the promise expressed here is not of a 'new Israel' but that the old Israel will not be destroyed. That the passage in its present form

[3] But see also Emmerson, *Hosea*, pp. 40.
[4] G. von Rad, *Old Testament Theology* II, ET Oliver & Boyd and Harper & Row 1965, pp. 144f.

points forward and that the Christ event may now be seen as the fulfilment of it is not to be doubted, as we shall see, but it cannot be held in this simplistic way.

There is, however, another way of interpreting these verses. The word translated *How* may introduce either a question, as in REB, or an exclamation as in II Sam. 1.19, 'How are the mighty fallen', A slightly stronger form of the word also occurs in Lam. 1.1 etc, expressing sorrow over the fate of Jerusalem. It is possible, therefore, that here in Hosea God is not questioning whether to carry out his sentence on Israel but is expressing sorrow that he must do so – 'How sad it is that I must give you up!' It thus expresses the dismay which God experiences at the punishment which must be meted out to Israel his son according to the law. *Admah* and *Zeboyim* are associated with Sodom and Gomorrah in destruction (Gen. 10.19; 41.2. 8; Deut. 29.33). The second half of v. 8 can be interpreted similarly. It is less emotional than the English translations suggest. 'Mind' is a better rendering than *heart*, and the fifth line then reads 'my mind is overturned upon me'. The last line reads literally 'Together my comfort grows warm', which does not make good sense. The Septuagint has: 'My heart is thrown into confusion.' Though we may not be sure about the exact meaning, it seems likely that here also Hosea meant to indicate that God was deeply troubled about the judgment he had had to make, as any father would be. It so happens that a similar passage in Jer. 31.20 anticipates the restoration of Israel alongside Judah (cf. also Ezek. 37.15). It is very possible, therefore, that in the seventh century or later preachers and prophets interpreted Hosea's words in this positive and hopeful sense. At that time, v. 9 could be added, completing the thought of God changing his mind and declining to carry out the proper sentence on his rebellious son. This suggestion that v. 9 is a later interpretation is reinforced by two other considerations. First, the second line may be translated 'I will not again *destroy Ephraim*'; (see RSV). The 'again' would hardly be applicable in the time of Hosea but it may be appropriate enough at a later date. Second, *Holy One* is a title for God which is used predominantly in literature which originates in Judah.

Whereas vv. 8–9 as presently understood mean that God would not carry out his sentence, vv. 10–11 indicate that he had already done so, or would do so, for they promise a return of those who have been deported to Assyria and Egypt. Many commentators share the view that v. 10, if not also v. 11, offers a later interpretation of Hosea's message, when it was used in Judah at a time when hopes were high that both Israel and Judah would be restored as the whole people of God again. Verse 12 clearly refers to Judah's idolatry. In any case, in the Hebrew Bible this is the opening verse of ch. 12, and so was not seen as following on directly from v. 11.

To sum up all this: since nowhere else in chs. 4–13 do we find any hope for Israel, and since chs. 1 and 3 as interpreted above express no hope from Hosea himself but only from a later period, it is most likely that Hosea regarded the punishment by death of Israel, YHWH's son, as essential, even though it caused YHWH much heart-searching. A later generation of preachers in Judah, using Hosea's words at a time when hopes were entertained of a new united Israel, interpreted the heart-searching more radically, and claimed that the destruction of the Northern Kingdom was not final. The sentence had been commuted and Israel would be restored along with Judah in a united kingdom. These hopes may well have arisen in the days of King Josiah (see notes on ch. 3). On this view there are at least two layers of meaning, the meaning the words had for Hosea and his contemporaries and the meaning they came to have for later Judaeans. It is not wrong, therefore, to see in the chapter the truth that God judges his children for disloyalty and disobedience; nor is it wrong to see the truth that God's love persists through human sin and judgment and in that sense the chapter prepares the way for the Christian gospel. There remains, however, in the New Testament and in Christian theology, a tension between God's judgment and his love. To lose sight of either is to impoverish the gospel. The text of Hosea 11 ensures that we do not.

Israel's treachery

11.12–12.1 As already stated, the final verse of ch. 11 in the English versions and the first verse of ch. 12 probably belong together. In the Hebrew Bible they are 12.1–2. They concern the *treachery* and *deceit* of Israel, and this is further defined by reference to alliances with *Assyria* and *Egypt*, an accusation we have met several times before and which reflects the reign of Hoshea after 732 BCE. 11.12 mentions *Judah* alongside Israel. We cannot be sure whether the last two lines of the verse are from Hosea or not. We saw earlier that both kingdoms were mentioned in that part of the book which seemed to reflect the Syro-Ephraimite alliance against Judah (5.8 – 6.6 at least). Judah's difficulties had been resolved when King Ahaz sought help from Assyria and so it is by no means impossible that these verses address the same situation. Others regard them as a later Judaean comment since they are more concerned with idolatry than with alliances.

Jacob past and present

12.2–14   The word *Judah* in 12.2 is much more likely to be the result of a change made when this part of Hosea's prophecy was later used in Judah, for the address is basically to the Northern Kingdom, and Hosea probably spoke to 'Israel' rather than to Judah. This would be parallel to *Jacob* in the following line. The whole passage remains difficult to interpret. Obviously Hosea was using the example of the patriarch Jacob to address the contemporary Israel. The uncertainty arises from the fact that we cannot be sure whether Hosea was accusing Israel of being as deceitful as the ancestor Jacob, or whether he was appealing to sinful Israel to change, just as Jacob had changed into Israel (Gen. 32.28). The structure of the passage may help us to decide. It is, once again, a legal disputation (cf. chs. 2 and 11), which opens with *a charge* being laid against the Israel of his day (v. 2). The indictment in vv. 3 and 4 is presented in terms of the patriarch's behaviour and this is followed (v. 5) by a hymn-like statement, not unlike part of those in the book of Amos (cf. Amos 4.13; 5.8; 9.6), which indicates who the God is with whom they have to deal. Next comes an appeal for a change of heart and direction (v. 6), followed by a further indictment (vv. 7 and 8) and the sentence (v. 9). Yet another indictment comes in vv. 10–13 and the sentence is confirmed in v. 14. If we see the passage as a whole and if this analysis is correct it seems to support the view that it constitutes more of a threat than an appeal. Now we must look at the detail.

The indictment in vv. 3–4 is based on three or possibly four episodes in the life of Jacob according to the tradition Hosea had received. We need to look at each of these separately before attempting an overall interpretation. First, *even in the womb Jacob supplanted his brother* clearly refers to the tradition of Jacob's birth in Gen. 25.22–26. When he and his twin Esau were born, Esau was born first but Jacob was grasping Esau's heel, seeking to hold him back. The name Jacob actually means 'he caught by the heel' or 'he supplanted' and the point is made clear in Gen. 27.36, where he is said by Esau to have 'supplanted' him twice. In this line, therefore, Jacob is seen in a bad light. Second, *in his manhood he strove with God, he strove with the angel and prevailed* picks up the incident at Penuel recorded in Gen. 32.22–32, which tells how Jacob's name ('supplanter') was changed to Israel (meaning 'strove with God'). As is often the case, the change in name corresponds to a change in character and this is why some commentators think that Hosea was here appealing for a similar change in the nation's character. The one line says Jacob *strove with God* and the other *he strove with the angel*. In the Genesis account we are told that it was 'a man' although it has just said Jacob was 'alone'. Perhaps the Hebrew simply means 'someone' and since he was alone the 'someone' may be thought to be a supernatural being. However, the man turns out to be God (v. 28). The narrator holds in suspense the identity of the assailant to heighten the sense of mystery. The same device is used in Gen. 18 of the visitor(s) to Abraham and Sarah. Hosea, therefore, seems to be following the tradition fairly closely. Further, in Gen. 32 there is some ambiguity as to who wins the contest. In vv. 25*a*, 26, and 28*b* Jacob appears to be winning, but in the final form of the story the assailant is victorious, for he demands to know Jacob's name (v. 27) while refusing to divulge his own (v. 29) and he puts Jacob's hip out of joint (v. 25). There is the same ambiguity in Hosea, for we cannot be sure who is the subject of the verb *prevailed*. The subject is included in the verb – 'he' *prevailed*. REB makes it appear that Jacob *prevailed*, but the 'he' may equally refer to *the angel* and this would fit better with the fact that Jacob *wept and entreated his favour*. In fact this last line does not occur in the Penuel tradition at all and must be Hosea's own comment, unless he has borrowed it from yet another Jacob tradition, namely that of his meeting with Esau after fleeing from his uncle Laban in Aram, where he wept (Gen. 33.4) and entreated his favour (Gen. 32.5). This interpretation of the lines in Hosea would suggest that Jacob was as guilty in his *manhood* as he was at birth and therefore Hosea's Israel is guilty of rebellion against God.

There has, however, been another interesting suggestion about

these two lines.[5] In v. 4 the Hebrew literally reads he *strove* towards
God, which does not make much sense. The preposition 'towards' in
Hebrew is *'ēl* and one of the names for God is *'ēl* and so it would be
possible to translate: 'God strove; the angel prevailed.' This does not
take us much further, but then the verb 'to strive; (*śrh*) is very similar
to the verb 'to rule' (*śrr*). Hosea is then thought to be making a play
on words. Isra-el means 'strove with God' because Jacob did so, but
then the first line of v. 4 should be translated 'God ruled: the angel
prevailed'. The arrangement of the line would be chiastic:

$$\begin{array}{ccc} \text{Ruled} & \diagdown & \text{God} \\ \text{The Angel} & \diagup & \text{prevailed} \end{array}$$

and this is a fairly common literary device. On this interpretation
Hosea would be appealing to contemporary Israel to be God-ruled,
that is, to change from *treachery* (11.12) and become submissive to
God's rule.

It is not easy to decide between these two interpretations. Perhaps
the former is to be preferred on the grounds of simplicity.

Lastly, *God met him at Bethel and spoke with him there* refers to Jacob's
dream at Bethel (Gen. 28). Again, the verbs have no subjects but REB
is right to supply *God*, though it could possibly mean that Jacob met
God there. The account in Genesis is straightforward enough but
there are some peculiarities about Hosea's words. In the first place
the verbs are not ordinary past tenses. They could be translated as
future or present but more likely they are intended to be frequentative
past: 'He used to meet him *at Bethel*.' Moreover the last line of v. 4 in
the Hebrew has the preposition 'us' instead of 'him'. The Septuagint
translated it 'him', probably seeking to make sense of it, and the
English versions have followed its lead. These two factors suggest,
however, a slightly different interpretation. Hosea was using the
tradition in a more subtle way than is usually thought. Certainly he
had Gen. 28 in mind but he was also thinking about the continuing
history of the shrine. Just as God met Jacob at Bethel so he used to
meet Israel there and there he used to speak to 'us', i.e. the continuing
Israel. In other words there was once a time when Bethel was all it
should have been, but now worship there was no longer acceptable
to God and God had withdrawn from meeting his people.

[5] L. M. Eslinger, 'Hosea 12.5*a* and Gen. 32.29: A Study in Inner Biblical Exegesis', *JSOT* 18, October 1980, pp. 91–99.

As we have seen, v. 5 looks like part of a hymn-like passage similar to those in Amos, drawing attention to YHWH, who is the true God of Bethel in contrast to the Baal they worshipped there.

Verse 6 is then an appeal to *turn back* to the proper conditions under which Bethel may again become a meeting place for God and Israel. Hosea realized they could not do this by themselves, as they had thought in 6. 1–3. They needed *God's help* in order to recover the *loyalty and justice* which would make it possible.

In spite of Hosea's appeal it seems clear from vv. 7 and 8 that it had no effect. Justice remained absent. In fact these two verses sound more like Amos than Hosea (cf. Amos 8.5). Only here does Hosea condemn the sins prevalent in social life such as cheating and growing rich at the expense of the poor. The passage refers to the *merchants* and the Hebrew word used by Hosea may also mean 'Canaanites'. Again he uses word play to show that the conduct of the Israelite traders was no better than that of the Canaanites from whom the land had been taken by God and entrusted to them. Yet there was no sense of *guilt* among them. *I have been the* LORD *your God since your days in Egypt* (v. 9) is almost a 'credal' statement which should have been the source of their confidence. Instead their confidence was all in themselves and their ability to get rich. Therefore, metaphorically. they must go back to the wilderness where they lived *in tents* (cf. 8. 13; 9.3; and Amos 3.2).

12.10–14   contain another indictment of Israel, using another Jacob tradition, that of his departure to Aram to work for Laban and find a wife. It is noticeable that REB leaves spaces between vv. 11 and 12, vv. 12 and 13, and vv. 13 and 14, suggesting a lack of continuity. RSV places v. 12 in parenthesis for the same reason and some commentators suggest moving v. 12, the verse about Jacob, to a position earlier in the chapter alongside the other Jacob references. The view taken here is that these five verses do form a coherent whole. The reason for this view is that all five verses are interlocked by language, style and content. First, vv. 10 and 13 are linked by references to prophets. Second, there is a verbal connection between *Gilgal* and *heaps of stones* in v. 11 and the word translated *bitter* in v. 14, as we shall see later. Third, vv. 11 and 12 are linked by *field* and *land*, both of which translate the same Hebrew word. Finally, vv. 12 and 13 are linked together by the repetition of the word *wife* in the Hebrew text of v. 12 (which reads more literally, 'Israel did service

159

for a wife, for a wife he tended sheep') and the repetition of *prophet* in v. 13 and by the contrasting statements *Jacob . . . tended sheep* and *Israel was tended*. So no verse can be removed without disturbing these connections, and the passage must be interpreted as a whole. J. L. Mays[6] is correct in seeing here a contrast between the prophetic movement of which Hosea was the current representative and the cult at Bethel established by Jacob and developed by Jeroboam I.

The passage opens with a verse about the prophetic movement (v. 10). The verb *spoke* is actually frequentative and should be translated 'I used to speak' as is shown by the phrase *vision after vision*. We have seen that this does not necessarily mean that they always saw visions (cf. the note on Amos 1.1), but they did *declare* God's *mind* (cf. Amos 3. 7). Hosea regarded Moses as the first in this line of prophets (v. 13) just as Deuteronomy saw him as the prophet *par excellence* (Deut. 18. 15–20). Under God Moses the *prophet brought Israel up from Egypt* (v. 13). By contrast *Jacob fled* from the promised land *to Aram* (Syria) and went into *service* to Laban *to win a wife* (v. 12; cf. Gen. 31). When Jacob eventually left Laban after serving fourteen years Laban caught up with him *in Gilead* (v. 11). There they made an agreement and sealed it by building an altar which, for Hosea, was no more than *heaps of stones*. They called on their respective gods to witness it (Gen. 31. 53). A heap of stones in Hebrew is *gal*, and so they called the place Gal-ed meaning 'heap of stones or "cairn" of witness'. The sacrifice on this altar to the two gods was seen by Hosea as idolatrous. The REB translation *sacrificed to bull-gods in Gilgal* is misleading, for the Hebrew simply says they offered cattle there. *Gilgal* also suggests a heap of stones (cf. Josh. 4) and is used for that reason. So (v. 14) contemporary Ephraim had provoked YHWH by erecting altars, except that the word 'altars' does not appear in REB. It uses the adjective *bitter*, but this is a rare word which occurs also in Jer. 31. 21, where REB translates it 'signpost' and where it is parallel with 'cairn' because signposts consisted of *heaps of stones*. So Hosea did not call them *'altars'* but 'signposts' because they were no more than *heaps of stones* similar to that used by Jacob and Laban. Therefore their blood guilt would remain with them and the scorn (*blasphemy*) with which they had treated him he would now show to them.

To recapitulate this difficult argument; Jacob had gone to Aram in search of a wife and worked as a servant to Laban. When he ran away

[6] Mays, *Hosea*, pp. 169ff.

and was overtaken by Laban they sacrificed to their gods on an altar which was nothing more than a heap of stones. Jacob's shrine at Bethel was now perpetuating this idolatry. Israel, the reformed Jacob, was then brought out of slavery in Egypt by Moses, the first of a line of prophets stretching down as far as Hosea himself, who therefore had the authority to condemn the cult at Bethel in spite of its Jacob connections. Like Amos therefore (Amos 7.10–14), Hosea also had to tackle the question of authority at the royal shrine of Bethel, and his final word was one of judgment.

The question is not a simple one of a dispute between the established religious orthodoxy manifest in the sanctuary and its priesthood, on the one hand, and the charismatic individual directly inspired and informed by God, on the other. It is extremely doubtful whether Hosea would have seen any essential contradiction between the two. Rather it is the failure of the former, its lapse into idolatry and its inability to recognize and acknowledge the God to whom the worship should be offered, which draws the criticism of the latter. It is one of the functions of those who stand in line with the prophets to comment on and be critical of the establishment when it loses its sense of direction.

Four oracles: Israel's rise and fall

13.1–16   This chapter consists of four originally separate and independent units placed side by side by the editor for whom they made up a whole.

13.1–3   This first saying looks to the past again (v. 1), turns to the present (v. 2) and threatens punishment in the future (v. 3) Although in Hosea *Ephraim* usually stands for the whole Northern Kingdom of Israel, here it refers to the tribe of that name and recalls its pre-eminence among all the Israelite tribes. *Ephraim*, along with Manasseh, was a son of Joseph, who himself was a prince or ruler over his brothers (Gen. 37.5–11). When Jacob blessed his grandsons priority was given to Ephraim (Gen. 48.17–20). The Joseph tribes more than any other are associated with the bondage in Egypt and the exodus, and when they settled in Canaan Ephraim in the central territory quickly established a leading position (Gen. 49.22–26; Deut. 33.13–17). Joshua was an Ephraimite (Josh. 24.30), and the covenant recorded in Josh. 24 took place in Ephraimite territory at Shechem. Moreover, Jeroboam I, the first king of the independent Israel, was an Ephraimite (I Kings 11.26). Such was Ephraim's pre-eminence that the name came to be used, especially by Hosea, for Israel as a whole. REB's translation of v. 1 is far better than NEB. RSV is still closer to the Hebrew, which seems to mean: 'When Ephraim spoke there was a trembling.' Such was the tribe's authority. We have no knowledge of any tradition associating the tribe with *Baal-worship* or describing its *death*. Perhaps in this last line of v. 1 Hosea began to think of the Northern Kingdom as a whole and to speak of it as being as good as dead on account of its worship of Baal. Verse 2 certainly moves on to the present. Jeroboam I had set up the bulls which came to be understood as images of Baal, but v. 2 suggests that these images have proliferated in Israel. The reference to *human sacrifice* is strange, to say the least, because Hosea has nowhere else mentioned it at the Northern shrines. It is hard to believe that he would have mentioned it only this once when he had so much to say about Israel's false worship. Nor is it mentioned in the historical book of II Kings at this time. Yet this is what the present text says. By a slight alteration of the Hebrew we may obtain the translation in RSV: 'Sacrifice to these, they say. Men kiss calves.' It seems more likely that this was Hosea's own meaning but the alteration to the present text did not come about simply by a copying error. It would have been deliberate. A century later than Hosea, and in Judah, when Josiah undertook his reforms he put an end to human sacrifice (II Kings 28.10), killing the priests and burning other human bones on the altar at Bethel (II Kings 23.15–20). It was very easy for anyone using Hosea's words at that time to make the slight change which would bring out their relevance even more clearly. Typically Hosea used four similes to describe how quickly the judgment will befall Israel. In 6.4 their loyalty had vanished like *morning mist* and *dew*. Here it is those things to which they have transferred their loyalty which would vanish.

13.4–8   The contrast set out in this short saying could hardly be more sharply drawn. The first three verses portray *the* LORD as their *saviour* from *Egypt* and the one who *cared for* them *in the wilderness*. We have met this recollection of Israel's past several times already and especially in chs. 2 and 11. The last two verses present him as *a wild beast* (four wild beasts in fact, *panther, leopard, she-bear* and *lioness*) about to *tear* Israel *apart*. Those who see Hosea as a more gentle prophet than Amos should pay attention to verses like these! The contrast between the *saviour* and the wild beasts is deliberate, for it focuses attention on that which brought about the change – *once satisfied, they grew proud, and so they deserted me*. Here in a nutshell is Hosea's basic message to his people. How typical it is to trust God when help is needed and forsake him when it is not!

13.9–11 It is customary to regard these verses as quite separate from the previous ones but it may be that the fierceness of Hosea's words in v. 8 evoked a sharp reaction from his audience, who could not believe what he had said to them. At any rate they seem to have been convinced that their national resources were sufficient to save them. Hosea's message was that the word of destruction had already been spoken – hence the past tense – *I have destroyed you*. The question, *who is there to help you*? is a rhetorical question; it is a denial that there is anyone who can help in the face of what YHWH had decreed. The same is true of the following questions. They need not imply that the monarchy had come to an end, but that the earthly *rulers* are powerless against YHWH. The request for a king in v. 10 may refer to the anointing of Saul (I Sam. 8.5), a request to which YHWH was said to have acceded reluctantly. So both the giving and the taking away of the king were acts performed in anger against Israel's lack of trust and loyalty to YHWH. The tenses of the verbs in v. 11, if they are past, must be frequentative and therefore this verse may well refer to the succession of kings following the death of Jeroboam II. Here again we are faced with the uncertainty as to whether Hosea was opposed to monarchy of any sort, monarchy of the Northern Kings, or the unstable monarchy in his own day.

13.12–16 The fourth saying in this chapter again threatens the most drastic punishment for Israel, and the final lines may suggest that the end of the Northern Kingdom is very near. Enough had already been said about *Ephraim's guilt* and so there was no need for Hosea to spell it out again. Here he was more concerned that their sins were on record and could not be expunged since they were written on *a scroll* and *tied up*. There they would be stored up for reference in any trial of Israel. The account of the birth of Ephraim in Gen. 41.52 makes no mention of anything like v. 13, so it is best to regard it simply

163

as a metaphor for the present people, who had refused every opportunity to turn back to YHWH and begin a new life. The language recalls that found in the Wisdom literature. An unborn child in the womb normally had the sense, literally 'wisdom' or 'know-how', to *present himself at the mouth of the womb at the proper time* and be born. Ephraim had lacked such wisdom. In a good deal of the Wisdom writings there is emphasis on things being done *at the proper* or right *time* in order for them to have a successful outcome (Eccles. 3.1–8). Israel's 'right time' had come and gone, and for lack of wisdom the opportunity had passed. The problem with v. 14 is that it can be understood either as a threat or as a promise, especially as the word *compassion* at the end of the verse is rendered by some as 'vengeance'. This word is found nowhere else in the Old Testament, but the verb from which it is derived is used and the most likely meaning of the word is *compassion*. The situation has been further complicated by the fact that St Paul quoted the verse in support of belief in the resurrection in I Cor. 15.55 and understood it to offer the promise of deliverance. If, however, we confine ourselves to the text and the context in Hosea it is virtually certain it is intended as a threat (so REB) which is continued in vv. 15–16. The change of metaphor from birth to death is sudden, except that a child which refused to be born may be thought of as dead. So the questions expect the answer 'No'. The words 'ransom' (here translated *deliver*) and *redeem* often lost much of their technical meaning, which involved the making of a payment, and they were frequently used more generally in the sense of *deliver*. They are used often of the deliverance from Egypt, but here of rescue from Sheol, the place where people go at death. All the Old Testament references to Sheol show it to be a place of meaningless existence which can in no way be described as life (cf. Job 7. 9f.; 10. 21f.; see also note on Amos 5. 4–6). *Death* and the *grave* ('Sheol') are therefore invited to produce the means to hold Ephraim in thrall. The threat is continued in v. 15 under the figure of the destructive *east wind*. The word *flourishes* is a play on the name Ephraim (cf. Gen. 41.52), which means 'to be fruitful', and *among his brothers* indicates Hosea's knowledge of the promises made to Joseph and Ephraim his son in Gen. 49.22–26 and Deut. 33.13–17. It may be that at the time when Hosea spoke these words the territory once allocated to Ephraim (Josh. 16.5–10) was all that was left of Northern Israel. The metaphor is then left behind and Hosea speaks directly of *the enemy* attack. The coming of the Assyrians was imminent and is described in the most terrible terms. For the ripping up of *pregnant women* cf. Amos 1. 13 and the note there. Such an action would ensure the end of the nation.

Repentance and restoration
Hosea 14.1–8

In this chapter there is a plea for repentance and confession of sin closely related to some of the sins condemned earlier by Hosea (vv. 1–3), followed by an oracle of salvation promising a glorious future (vv. 4–7). There follows a single verse (8), which was probably separate from the preceding verses even though it, too, offers promise. Finally the book ends with a call to readers to listen to what it says. These may have been four independent units, but they have been carefully placed together in this combination by the editor of the book.

14.1–3   There are no safe grounds for regarding this saying as spoken by anyone other than Hosea. The language and the subject matter are what we have grown accustomed to. For the most part Hosea had condemned the sins mentioned here but there were occasions when he saw the possibility of change, at least theoretically. In 5.15 there had been a threat *until in remorse they seek me*, and so Hosea may well have been willing to appeal for repentance, even if he thought it to be unlikely. The repentance, though, would have to go much deeper and more sincere than that in 6.1–3. It must be with *confession* and commitment to change. *We shall pay our vows* may equally well mean 'we shall pay as compensation', making good their sins. Verse 3 would be an acknowledgment that reliance on *Assyria* is useless and a promise not to worship man-made idols. The *horses* may refer to military strength in general or, in the light of Isa. 31.1. to Egyptian help. Instead, they must confess their trust in the *compassion* of YHWH.

14.4–7   In the context of worship a confession of sin was followed by an oracle of salvation and some explain the linkage of this section to the previous one in the light of this. It should be noted, however, that there is not a hint that Israel took any notice of Hosea's appeal, nor does the salvation saying make any reference to Israel's confession or change. The emphasis is solely on YHWH's free grace – *I shall love them freely. Heal*, of course, was a word on Hosea's lips more than once, but in view of the fact that he spoke almost exclusively of Israel's defeat and destruction, even in 13.12–16, it is more than likely that this promise of restoration comes from a later time. It is probably a Judaean preacher's view of the response of YHWH to the events of the exile in Babylon. Very simply, God will *heal* their *apostasy*, and will grant them fertility. Such views are common in Isa. 40–55 and in the latter part of Ezekiel. The first line of v. 7 may be translated literally 'They will return who dwell in his shadow'. This may well be correct and, if it is, then the verse appears to promise a return from exile. We have already seen that a hope of Israel's return alongside Judah was a feature of prophecy at that time (Ezek. 37.15ff.) and the belief was that there would be a prosperous united kingdom.

14.8   This is the only place in the Old Testament where YHWH's relationship with Israel is portrayed as a *tree that shelters* them. It is possible that use was being made of a myth of the sacred tree which provides fertility (cf. the tree of life in Gen. 2.9,24). There may be some support for this in that the Hebrew words behind *declare* and *affirm* closely resemble the names of well-known Near Eastern goddesses, Anath and Asherah. As usual with the prophets their use of a myth does not imply belief in it; it simply provides a useful means of conveying a message. The verse calls the nation *Ephraim* as Hosea so frequently does. Once we remove the verse from its present context and examine it on its own, it looks like a typical warning from Hosea against idolatry and a call to rely on YHWH, who provides his people with *prosperity* (cf. ch.2).

By placing the verse here, though, the editor has changed its significance. Now both vv. 4–7 and v. 8 are seen as the consequence of penitence and confession to which YHWH responds with *prosperity* and abundance. The fact that this comes from an editor rather than from Hosea himself does not in any way diminish its importance or its relevance to us. It remains a valuable insight into the nature of God which finds fuller confirmation in the New Testament.

Concluding advice

14.9 This final verse of the book is the concluding advice of the editor to the reader. It is couched in the language of the Wisdom literature and it makes three points which we do well to heed. First, it speaks of the need for wisdom in reading and interpreting the book – and we could all agree with that! Second and implicitly, such wisdom requires as its starting point 'fear of the LORD' (Job 28.28; Prov. 1. 7). In other words the reader who wishes to understand must share the faith, the reverence, the obedience to YHWH, which is characteristic of his prophets. Those who are *righteous walk* in *the LORD's way* but *sinners stumble*. Third, the verse makes it quite clear that the words of Hosea had relevance not only to the people whom Hosea actually addressed but that they were meant to be understood and used and applied to new situations as they arose. This is still the task of the Christian preacher and teacher, who must do all in his power to grasp Hosea's message to the eighth-century Israelites, but who must also keep his eyes and ears open for what the words of both Hosea himself and the editor mean for his own contemporary generation. It is hoped that this commentary will go some way towards helping in that task.

Even more it will need commitment to the God of Hosea, who was also the God and Father of Jesus Christ and who disclosed himself more fully through him to everyone who had eyes to see and ears to hear.